Contents

Introduction   1

1 Animal Learning: No Match for Human Learning   13

2 Tool-use and Tool-making: Do Primates Have
   'Culture'?   33

3 'Folk Physics': Do Apes Understand How Tools Work? 28

4 'Folk Psychology': Are Apes Able to Think About
   Others' Perceptions, Intentions, Desires and Beliefs?   45

5 Language and Communication   79

6 Evolution and Consciousness   95

   Conclusion: Celebrating the Achievements of
   Humanity   109

   Bibliography   115

   Index   126

Just Another Ape?

Helene Guldberg

SOCIETAS
essays in political
& cultural criticism

imprint-academic.com

Published by
Imprint Academic, PO Box 200, Exeter EX5 5YX, UK

Published in the USA by Societas
Imprint Academic, Philosophy Documentation Center
PO Box 7147, Charlottesville, VA 22906-7147, USA

A CIP catalogue record for this book is available from the
British Library and US Library of Congress

ISBN 9781845401634

Acknowledgements

I would like to thank Anthony Haynes for encouraging me to write this book. Special thanks also go to Dolan Cummings, Jeremy Taylor and Jim Butcher for reading initial drafts of the entire book and giving me invaluable and detailed feedback. Others have been helpful by reading drafts of particular chapters and drawing my attention to useful material, including Jennie Bristow, Jan Bowman, Claire Fox, Rob Lyons, Brendan O'Neill and my husband Patrick.

Introduction

'Homo sum: humani nil a me alienum puto.' ('I am human: nothing human is alien to me')

Terentius Lucanus, (ca.195BC–159BC)

Today we are continually reminded about the damage done to our planet and its many living species by 'selfish', 'greedy' and 'predatory' humans. Everyone from celebrity chefs and supermodels to politicians and the media chatterati is getting hot under the collar about our treatment of animals – whether tigers in India, pandas in China, gorillas in Africa, seals in Canada, polar bears in the North Pole, whales in international waters, or indeed chickens in the UK.

When I started writing *Just Another Ape?*, the plight of chickens was the latest *cause célèbre*. Celebrity chef Hugh Fearnley-Whittingstall launched the campaign 'Chicken Out' in 2008 to try to stop supermarkets from stocking factory-farmed chicken, and in the world of the ethical food-snob, 'cheap meat' became synonymous with barbarism. Before that, luxury goods were the focus of complaint: veal calves, *foie gras*, and, of course, fur. Supermodels Cindy Crawford, Linda Evangelista and Naomi Campbell made headlines in the 1990s by posing naked for the campaign by People for the Ethical Treatment of Animals (PETA),'I'd rather go naked than wear fur', only to be seen a few years later on the catwalk wearing fur coats, the fun of principled nudity apparently having worn off.

A few years later celebrity artist Rolf Harris made an acid-techno single about Canada's annual seal hunt, titled 'Slaughter on the Ice', calling on us all to 'rid the world of this shocking annual bloodbath.' Drawing attention to the plight of animals further from home, Hollywood actors Minnie Driver and Ralph Fiennes, along with countless other celebrities, have taken part in television commercials for the US conservation group WildAid, warning of the many perils faced by Asia and Africa's endangered species. The United Nations named 2009 the Year of the Gorilla 'to save one of humankind's closest but critically endangered relatives' (UN News Centre, 2008).

And let's not forget the polar bear, which, as Brendan O'Neill points out on *spiked*, has become 'a symbolic victim of man's wanton destruction of the planet' and 'the poster boy for the green lobby'(O'Neill, 2008). In the May 2007 issue of *Vanity Fair*, Leonardo DiCaprio posed with the polar bear cub Knut on an Icelandic glacier (with a little help from PhotoShop) in order to highlight what might be lost as a result of manmade global warming.

Human beings are 'heartless exploiters of animals', and have 'a sentimental tendency to put [our] own species on a pedestal' exploiting other animals 'as our slaves', warns Richard Ryder (6 August 2005), British psychologist and philosopher and former chair of the Royal Society for the Prevention of Cruelty to Animals (RSPCA). Ryder is the man who coined the term 'speciesism', which, he says, came to him in 1970 while lying in a bath in Oxford. Speciesism is 'like racism or sexism – a prejudice based upon morally irrelevant physical differences', he explains (Ryder, 6 August 2005).

'Speciesism' has since been popularised by the world-renowned Australian philosopher Peter Singer. Singer co-founded the Great Ape Project (GAP) in 1993 because of the 'undeniable scientific proof that non-human great apes share more than genetically similar DNA with their human counterparts' (GAP, 1993). He argues that we need to 'break the species barrier' and extend rights to apes, in the first instance, followed by all other animal species. Singer is far from alone in wanting to knock human beings off our 'anthropocentric pedestal': those who argue that animals, and especially apes, are really 'just like us' are getting an ever-wider hearing today.

Even Spain, the land famous for bullfights, is taking up the issue of animal rights: in March 2009, 100 Spaniards stripped naked, smeared themselves in red liquid and lay on the ground in a Madrid square as part of an international day of protest against Canada's annual 'massacre' of seals; and in 2008 the Spanish parliament announced its support for the Great Ape Project's mission to give apes legal rights currently only granted to human beings. 'This is a historic day in the struggle for animal rights and in defence of our evolutionary comrades which will doubtless go down in the history of humanity,' Pedro Pozas, the Spanish director of the Great Apes Project, said (Glendinning, 2008).

Meanwhile, a recent *New York Times* op-ed took issue with the degrading use of chimps in advertising. Representations of chimpanzees 'serve as a benchmark for our society's moral progress', claimed the *New York Times*, but conceded that misrepresentations 'may not be as repugnant as racism, bigotry or sexism' (Ross, 2008). Readers were encouraged not to lose heart: the 'good news' is that 'a growing number of companies, including Honda, Puma and Subaru, have pledged to stop the use of primates in advertisements' (Ross, 2008).

In contrast, three decades ago, when Singer's book *Animal Liberation* – often referred to as the Bible of the animal rights movement – was first published, the intellectual and public mood was very different (Singer, 1975). The use of the term 'speciesism', drawing explicit parallels with racism and sexism, provoked widespread ridicule. It was considered insulting and offensive to equate the plight of animals with the social inequalities that had given rise to the civil rights movements of the previous decades. But according to Singer, the term was used deliberately, 'to say that just as we needed to overcome prejudices against black people, women and gays, so too we should strive to overcome our prejudices against non-human animals and start taking their interests seriously' (Singer, 2003).

In his 2007 book *Ten Questions Science Can't Answer (Yet!)*, Michael Hanlon, science editor of the *Daily Mail*, similarly draws parallels between speciesism and racism. He writes:

> It may well be the case that in decades or centuries to come we may look back upon the way we treat our fellow creatures today with the same sort of revulsion with which we now treat slavery – a practice which 250 years ago was widely accepted in most of the 'advanced' societies on the planet (Hanlon, 2007: 40).

Today the assertion that the interests of animals' should be considered on a par with those of humans rarely raises an eyebrow. Indeed, a recent op-ed in the *New York Times* argued: 'This idea popularized by Professor Singer – that we have ethical obligations that transcend our species – is one whose time appears to have come' (Kristof, 2009). As Singer points out in the introduction to his book *In Defense of Animals:* 'In 1970 the number of writings on the ethical status of animals was tiny [and] the tally now must be in the thousands' (Singer, 2006: 2).

To me, this growing obsession with animal welfare tells us more about what the protagonists think of human beings than what they think of chickens, seals, whales, polar bears, tigers, apes or any other beast. Today's sentimentalised view of animals is more often than not coupled with a nightmarish vision of human destructiveness – and in many cases revealing a rather degraded view of particular classes and races of people.

Food snobs hide behind a concern for the welfare of chickens to have a go at the uncouth masses who buy their cheap chicken in Tesco. Wildlife conservationists in Africa have a long history of being widely disliked by the local community because of their often outspoken racism and violence against the local people. And the anti-whaling lobby – with Britain, Australia and New Zealand at the helm – uses moral grandstanding as a way of having a go at the 'uncivilised' whale-eating nations of the world, and presenting themselves as pure and righteous in comparison. They are clearly not driven by anti-hunting sentiments in general as in all these countries people kill other animals for their meat and fur.

But it is not only a matter of celebrity chefs, TV personalities, supermodels, actors and politicians cynically jumping on the fashionable animal welfare bandwagon to puff themselves up and feed their own sense of superiority. Today's obsession with animal welfare indicates a broader contempt for humanity in general. *Times* columnist Matthew Parris sums up this outlook well: 'To many, love of "Nature" is the flipside of distaste of Man, or an embarrassment – even shame – about being human' (Parris, 2008).

In *The Great Ape Project* Douglas Adams, of *Hitchhiker's Guide to the Galaxy* fame, describes his thoughts while watching free-living gorillas in Zaire. It is 'patronising' to presume to judge their intelligence 'as if our own was any kind of standard by which to measure', he writes (Adams, 1993: 22).

Human beings are constantly denigrated. Some even portray humans as aggressive cancerous cells destroying all other life on Earth. Back in 1992 the American physician and fossil researcher Professor Jerold Lowenstein wrote in the US science and technology magazine *Discover*:

> We are infecting the planet, growing recklessly as cancer cells do, destroying Gaia's other specialized cells (that is, extinguishing other species), and poisoning our air supply (Lowenstein, 1 November 1992).

The next logical step is to call for the destruction of these 'cancerous cells': in other words, the elimination of humans. Indeed, some prominent philosophers, scientists, social scientists, novelists and aristocrats have taken that logical next step. On becoming a patron of the Optimum Population Trust, David Attenborough warned that the recent increase in human population was having a devastating effect on ecology and pollution. 'I've never seen a problem that would be easier to solve with fewer people, or harder, and ultimately impossible, with more', he said (Bahra, 2009). Queen Elizabeth's husband, Prince Philip, renowned for his often racist gaffes suggests how he could help reduce the human footprint: 'If I were reincarnated, I would wish to be returned to Earth as a killer virus to lower human population levels', he says (Marquardt, 1995: 3).

John Gray, Professor of European Thought at the London School of Economics, shows a similar lack of concern about whether humans have a future on Earth – it is the balance of the world's ecosystem that we should really be worried about, he argues. In *Straw Dogs*: *Thoughts on humans and other animals*, he writes:

> Homo rapiens (*sic*) is only one of very many species, and not obviously worth preserving. Later or sooner, it will become

extinct. When it is gone the Earth will recover. Long after the last traces of the human animal have disappeared, many of the species it is bent on destroying will still be around, along with others that have yet to spring up. The Earth will forget mankind. The play of life will go on (Gray, 2002: 151).

Sharing a panel with Gray, psychologist Susan Blackmore said on BBC Radio 3's *Nightwaves*: 'For the planet's sake, I hope we have bird flu or some other thing that will reduce the population, because otherwise we're doomed.'

In May 2008 Channel 4's *Life After People* dramatised what would happen to our planet if humans were to vanish overnight. Orange-prize winning author Lionel Shriver applauded this 'marvellous documentary', writing in the *Daily Telegraph*:

> In time, all the unpleasant effects of our filthy, meddling, too-successful race subside. Surviving cattle multiply, and run the plains in droves. "Endangered" tigers and rhinos thrive. Flora and fauna tangle over former cropland. Seas are replenished – the North Sea has cod – until the lush, teeming planet is returned to an Eden of plenty and natural balance (Shriver, 2008).

She concludes:

> [T]he vision at the end of the documentary of burgeoning forests bounding with bears is strangely uplifting. If we want to stick around, we'll have to keep from defecating where we eat. But if we make a mess of matters and disappear, another form of life will take our place – creatures beautiful, not so self-destructive, or simply weird. That's cheerful news, really (Shriver, 2008).

Non-human animals are presented as pure and serene in comparison with egotistical and destructive humans. The Danish former air hostess, Lone Drøscher Nielsen, who now runs one of the world's largest primate rescue centre in Borneo, told *Scanorama* magazine:

> I wonder whether Darwin had it all backwards. Nothing as innocent, beautiful and glorious as the orangutan could possibly have evolved into man (Desilets, 2008).

This notion of the human race as a problem – or even a pest – is increasingly mainstream. But having said that, very few people actually live their lives on the basis of this outlook. In fact, most people would find it abhorrent if we were to treat human beings as if they were of lesser value than animals. Take the 2007 case of the mother who left her three-year-old daughter, Tiffany Wright, to starve to death alone in a filthy bug-infested bedroom above a pub, while showing more concern for her pet dog. The revelation that she had worried about the health of her dog, but not at all about her own daughter, disgusted many people. Alan Goldsack QC said in court to the dead girl's mother: 'One almost unbelievable piece of evidence is that on what was probably Tiffany's last day alive, you were discussing on the phone concerns you had about one of your dog's weight and feeding problems'.

Apart from a few eccentrics, the vast majority of people value human life above animal life. We go about our daily lives viewing human beings as special and qualitatively different from animals. However, the problem is that it is considered outrageously arrogant to assert this superiority.

As the medical scientist Raymond Tallis points out 'our achievements and abilities are continually denigrated by anthropomorphising or "Disneyfying" what animals do and "animalomorphising" what human beings get up to' (Tallis, 2003). On the one hand, nature programmes continually foist human characteristics upon animals – with commentators breathlessly telling us about love, jealousy and intrigue, or hate, grief and revenge in the animal kingdom. On the other hand, we are told that our behaviour is determined by our genetic make-up, with our essentially Stone Age brains being hard-wired to deal only with challenges of our evolutionary past. As American journalist and blogger Steve Sailer points out in the American magazine *National Review*: 'Looking for insight into human nature by studying our closest relatives in the evolutionary tree, our fellow primates, has become a popular intellectual pastime. For guidance on how to live, we increasingly look less to scriptures and more to our cousins with the low foreheads' (Sailer, 1999).

John Gray is in a sense right when he claims in *Straw Dogs* that the important battle today is between humanists and those who argue that 'humans can no more be masters of their destiny than any other animal' (Gray, 2002: 4). Unfortunately few humanists are throwing very many punches today. As a result we have taken quite a beating.

'So what?', you may think: 'it's about time human beings took a knock or two: we have placed ourselves at the centre of the universe for long enough'. Does it really matter if humanity is presented in a bad light? I believe it does: it matters because this degraded view of human beings is not only depressing, but fatalistic and harmful.

Today's misanthropic cultural outlook – one that continually denigrates humans, blurs the differences between humans and other animals, and is not prepared to put the case first and foremost for human interests – has negative consequences for how we live our lives and how we organise society. Most importantly, without a belief in human uniqueness, there cannot be a belief in the possibility of changing the world for the better.

But also, look at the ongoing controversy surrounding animal research. In the past few years in the UK, animal rights activists have succeeded in blocking a primate research centre at Cambridge University, and interrupting work at an animal research facility at Oxford University. The response from government ministers in the face of the protests by anti-vivisectionists was to argue that the UK has the 'strongest laws in the world' on the use of animals in research and stressing that animal welfare is 'paramount'.

The government cannot bring itself to argue for the importance of these research centres on the basis of *human* interest. In fact, defensively voicing concern for the welfare of animals will not convince anybody and most certainly will not allay public unease about animal research. For how can we justify the use of millions of animals in experiments to further scientific knowledge and save human lives – experiments that include cutting animals open, pumping them full of toxins and carcinogens, and ultimately 'destroying' them – unless we believe, and are willing to argue, that human beings are morally more valuable than animals?

Many major medical advances – insulin to treat diabetes, polio vaccines, antibiotics, safe anaesthetics, open heart surgery, organ transplantation, drug treatments for ulcers, asthma and high blood pressure, and much more – would not have been won, or would have been introduced at great human cost, if it were not for animal experimentation. There are few people alive today who won't have benefited in some way from such medical advances.

So long as animal research helps in the battle against disease and disability, thereby improving human welfare, it should be championed as a morally good pursuit – without feeling the need to apologise for anything. Professor Colin Blakemore, one of the few British scientists who has consistently spoken out in favour of animal research, told the *New Statesman* in 2008 that animal research is 'the most noble thing we do to animals' (Byrnes, 28 February 2008).

Of course, some people are more squeamish than others and may find the reality of what goes on in animal research labs upsetting. But that is tough. Animal research cannot be soft and cuddly, and because it is necessary for scientific advance – now and for the foreseeable future – it must continue. We cannot dodge the fact that the killing and maiming of animals in experiments is necessary to advance human knowledge and to improve medical science.

Similarly the factory farming of animals – which makes meat–production more efficient and cost-effective – is far from unethical. Surely a more efficient way of feeding the world's population should be celebrated rather than damned? In more advanced urban societies most of us have the luxury of not witnessing first-hand the brutality of life for many farm animals – nor the brutality of nature for that matter, described by the English poet Alfred Lord Tennyson as 'red in tooth and claw'. Many therefore find images of chickens cooped up in cages, seals clubbed to death or turtles being de-shelled distressing. But the fact that something isn't pretty doesn't make it morally wrong. People need to eat, and we feed ourselves through farming. Nobody is forcing celebrity chefs to buy cheap chickens if they don't want to; by the same token, celebrity chefs should be careful how they guilt-trip people for whom food is not a 'lifestyle choice', but a matter of everyday sustenance and grocery bills.

The argument for human and animal equivalence is at its strongest in relation to our closest living relatives – the great apes. In his 2009 book *Not a Chimp*, science documentary film producer Jeremy Taylor raises some important questions:

> Why is it that human uniqueness has become such a shameful idea? Is it that we, as laymen, simply cannot prevent our innate ability to anthropomorphise chimps from cloaking them in our cognitive clothes? Is it that we, as biologists, are so petrified of creationists that we not only stress the biological continuum between us and chimpanzees, but seem to find it obligatory to collapse that distance into close proximity? Does it involve an exaggeration of the sagacity and wisdom of chimps, a loss of confidence in where the power of human intellect has got us, or both? (Taylor, 2009: 9).

In *Just Another Ape?* I focus on the differences between human beings and apes – to show just how exceptional humans really are. It is an argument that needs to be put across – not only because it is historically and scientifically correct (even if 'politically incorrect'), but because unless we have faith in our own abilities, society will stagnate. As the philosopher Simon Blackburn told me: 'the prevailing sentimentalism, and sheer dotty thinking about the relation between human and animal capacities [and the] distorted understandings of the similarities and differences, needs a good shake-up'.

I hope this book will play a part in doing just that.

Chapter One
Animal Learning: No Match for Human Learning

'The proper study of mankind is man.'
Alexander Pope, An Essay on Man, *1733.*

Peter Singer, the 'father' of the animal rights movement, claims that the great apes - that is orang-utans, gorillas, chimpanzees and bonobos - are not only our closest living relatives, but are also beings who possess many of the characteristics that have long been considered distinctive to humans (Singer, 2003). A number of internationally renowned scientists and primatologists have joined Singer in calling for a United Nations Declaration of the Rights of Great Apes. 'We demand the extension of the community of equals to include all great apes: human beings, chimpanzees, gorillas and orang-utans', they write (Cavalieri & Singer, 1993: 4). Among the principles or rights that should be 'enforceable by law', are 'the right to life', 'the protection of individual liberty' and the 'prohibition of torture' (Cavalieri & Singer, 1993: 4).

One of the signatories of the Great Ape Project (GAP), Deborah Fouts, co-director of the Chimpanzee and Human Communication Institute, argues: '[Chimpanzees] are a people. Non-human, but definitely persons. They haven't built a rocket ship to the moon. But we're not that different' (Keim, 2008).

In the 1993 book *The Great Ape Project,* put together by Singer and the Italian philosopher Paola Cavalieri, Douglas

Adams describes the human-like characteristics of free-living gorillas in Zaire:

> They look like humans, they move like humans, they hold things in their fingers like humans, the expressions which play across their faces and in their intensely human-looking eyes are expressions which we instinctively feel we recognise as human expressions (Adams, 1993: 21).

The Great Ape Project (GAP) emphasises our genetic similarity to the great apes, in particular to chimpanzees, with whom we share more than 98 percent of our DNA. It is estimated that humans and chimps originated from a common ancestor only six million years ago. One might therefore assume that there will be a high degree of mental as well as genetic similarity with these close cousins.

But how human-like are they? Much of what we have learnt about the great apes in the wild is from the work of the three women dubbed 'Leakey's Angels'- Jane Goodall, Dian Fossey and Biruté Galdikas. They were all encouraged and funded by the world renowned paleontologist Louis Leakey. Jane Goodall spent 30 years living with chimpanzees in Tanzania. Dian Fossey observed gorillas in the mountain forests of Rwanda on a daily basis for 18 years. And Biruté Galdikas has conducted the longest continuous study of orang-utans – more than 30 years - in Indonesian Borneo.

Jane Goodall made a significant breakthrough by showing that chimpanzees not only use but also make tools - using sticks to fish for termites, stones as anvils or hammers, and leaves as cups or sponges. In her book *Through a Window: thirty years with the chimpanzees of Gombe* she recounts writing to Louis Leakey about her first observations, 'describing how [the chimpanzee] David Greybeard not only used bits of straw to fish for termites but actually stripped leaves from a stem and thus *made* a tool (Goodall, 1990: 15). She writes:

> And I remember too receiving the now oft-quoted telegram he sent in response to my letter: 'Now we must redefine tool, redefine man, or accept chimpanzees as humans' (Goodall, 1990: 15).

According to the *New Yorker,* Goodall 'has taken her place as a world authority': 'By dint of heroic patience and labour in the accumulation of verifiable data, she has substantiated her once startling revelations – that chimpanzees think, and can reason out simple problems; [...] that they know love and jealousy, grief and boredom; and that they will murder and make war' (Goodall, 1990: back cover).

She laments that when she began her study at Gombe in 1960 'it was not permissible – at least not in ethological circles – to talk about an animal's mind'. But she refused to succumb to scientific rigour. Breaking the mould in primate studies, she gave all the chimps names, talked about their 'minds' and 'personalities' and described their behaviour in terms of motivation and purpose. She writes:

> Often I have gazed into a chimpanzee's eyes and wondered what was going on behind them. I used to look into Flo's, she so old [*sic*], so wise. What did she remember of her young days? David Greybeard had the most beautiful eyes of them all, large and lustrous, set wide apart. They somehow expressed his whole personality, his sense of self-assurance, his inherent dignity – and from time to time, his utter determination to get his own way (Goodall, 1990: 10).

Dian Fossey followed in Jane Goodall's footsteps and named most of the gorillas that she observed. She established the Karisoke Research Center in Rwanda in 1967 and on a daily basis for almost two decades would sit within a few feet of the gorillas observing their behaviour. In her book *Gorillas in the Mist* she writes:

> My research studies of this majestic and dignified great ape – a gentle yet maligned nonhuman primate – have provided insight to the essentially harmonious means by which gorillas organize and maintain their familial groups and also have provided understanding of some of the intricacies of various behavioural patterns never previously suspected to exist (Fossey, 1983: xv).

She managed to gain the trust of the gorillas, and get close to them, by adopting some of their behaviours and vocalisations: she would imitate the gorillas' scratching, copy their grunts and belch vocalisations and adopt their knuckle-walking style. She even tried chest-beating, but soon realised this was not a good idea as it is a sign of alarm and excitement. Appearing on the front-cover of *National Geographic* in 1970 'launched her into instant celebrity, forever changing the image of the gorillas from dangerous beasts to gentle beings', The Dian Fossey Gorilla Fund International (DFGFI) website boasts.

After finding one of her favourite gorillas, Digit, decapitated, on new years day in 1978, Fossey declared war on the local poachers. DFGFI admits that Fossey fought poachers 'through unorthodox methods': she even took the 10-year old son of a local poacher hostage. She called her tactics – which included organised anti-poaching patrols and placing bounties on poachers heads – 'active conservation'. In 1985 she was brutally murdered in her cabin in the base camp in Rwanda. An unknown attacker had split her skull open with a machete, a tool used by many poachers in the area. She had confiscated the machete a few years earlier and had hung it – like a trophy – on the wall of her living room next to her bedroom.

Biruté Galdikas, who has succeeded in making a name for herself as a world expert in orang-utans, is another angel who has featured on the front cover of *National Geographic*. Like the two other angels, she has conflated field primatology with conservations issues. Alongside carrying out daily observations, she has been campaigning relentlessly to save orang-utans and the forests they inhabit, and to bring the plight of this ape to the attention of the world. In *Reflections of Eden: My years with the orangutans of Borneo* she writes: 'I have always felt strongly that saving orang-utans is as important as studying them' (Galdikas, 1995: 5).

Again, like Goodall and Fossey, Galdikas refused to be shackled by scientific principles and standards, and instead described the apes in human terms. Referring to one orang-utan, recognised by Galdikas as a 'kindred spirit', she writes: 'Akmad was a lady. She has a gentle way about her. She never ran, she always walked. She never grabbed, she always reached. Even her squeal had a daintiness that the vocalizations of other orangutans lacked. How human she appeared, like an orange gnome, with her intelligent quietly inquisitive face' (Galdikas, 1995: 7).

In her book *Orangutan Odyssey* she argues that orangutans are 'the best mothers in the world' (Galdikas, 1999). She told *CBS news* in 1999: 'We're dealing with a species that is much older than ourselves – a species that reflects what we were before we became human. I suddenly realized I had reached the point where it was hard for me to see the differences between apes and humans' (*CBS News* July 14, 1999).

The writings of 'Leakey's angels' are littered with anthropomorphism – the attribution of human characteristics to animals – and all three women have rejected what they see as the straight-jacket of scientific rigour. They have not shown any recognition of the need to question and test their own assumptions. Instead they have gone with their gut instincts when trying to understand what goes on inside the heads of these beasts.

The problem is that this can be very deceptive. It is of course quite hard for human beings *not* to ascribe human emotions and human motivations to animal behaviour, but it is precisely for this reason we need to ensure our presumption are properly tested.

An interesting recent experiment carried out by Alexandra Horowitz at Barnard College in New York showed how easy it is to be led astray by anthropomorphic thinking. Horowitz showed that dog owners' attribution of understanding and human-like emotions to their pets was completely unwarranted (Horowitz, 2009). The dog owners were utterly convinced that they could tell by their dog's 'guilty look' whether or not the dog had done something it had been told not to do. In fact, the experiment showed these apparent 'guilty' looks had nothing to do with 'guilt'.

Horowitz' experiment involved getting 14 owners to show their dogs a biscuit and instruct the dogs not to eat it. The owners were then asked to leave the room and while they were gone Horowitz either allowed the dogs to eat the biscuit or she removed it. In some trials she told the owners that their dog had been disobedient and eaten the treat; in others, she told them their dog had done as instructed and left the treat uneaten. What the owners were told did not necessarily correspond with reality, however. The results showed no relationship between the dogs' 'guilty look' and whether or not the dogs had in fact eaten the treat. Instead the dogs looked most 'guilty' if they were admonished by their owners for eating the treat when they in fact *hadn't* done so. 'These results indicate that a better description of the so-called "guilty look" is that it is a response to owner cues, rather than that it shows an appreciation of a misdeed', Horowitz wrote (Horowitz, 2009: 447). One therefore needs to look beyond first impressions in order to establish what animals do or do not 'know' and to uncover whether or not they are capable of feeling human-like emotions like guilt.

While many people have always been sceptical of dog owners' claims about the human-like intelligence of their pets, the idea that apes might have minds somewhat like our own is much more widespread among scientists as well as animal-lovers. There is good reason to doubt this too, however. Daniel Povinelli, director of the Cognitive Evolution Group at the University of Louisiana at Lafayette, has carried out some ground-breaking research to compare and contrast how humans and chimpanzees understand the world around them, which has led him to challenge the idea that primates think anything like humans. He writes:

> After several decades of being fed a diet heavy on exaggerated claims of the degree of mental continuity between humans and apes, many scientists and laypersons alike now find it difficult to confront the existence of radical differences, as well. But then, in retrospect, how viable was the idea of seamless mental continuity in the first place? After all, it tended to portray chimpanzees as watered-down humans, not-quite-finished children. Despite the fact that this notion can be traced straight to Darwin, it is an evolutionarily dubious proposition, to say the least (Povinelli, 2004: 31).

In March 2009 the *Guardian* reported on 'the loutish behaviour of a stone-throwing chimpanzee at a zoo near the Arctic circle', which apparently challenges scientists' belief that humans are unique (Sample, 2009). The discovery that the aggressive chimp had gathered stones over a period of time, in order to throw them later on at unsuspecting spectators – implying some kind of forethought and planning – astounded many scientists.

Mathias Osvath of Lund University in Sweden wrote in the journal *Current Biology*: 'Such planning implies advanced consciousness and cognition traditionally not associated with non-human animals' (Osvath, 2009). He argued that the behaviour of the stone-thrower shows that chimps 'have a highly developed consciousness, including life-like mental simulations of potential events': 'When wild chimps collect stones or go out to war, they probably plan this in advance. I would guess that they plan much of their everyday behaviour.' The science editor of *The Times*, Mark Henderson reported that even some primatologists were surprised by these revelations about the apparent degree of chimp intelligence (Henderson, 2009).

A few days later *BBC News* reported on a study published in the *International Journal of Primatology*, which uncovered novel tool-using abilities among wild chimpanzees in central Africa: 'Cameras have revealed how "armed" chimpanzees raid beehives to gorge on sweet honey', the BBC reported. Scientists found that the primates 'crafted large clubs from branches to pound the nests until they broke open' (*BBC News*, 2009).

Some claim that chimps may even outstrip humans in some aspects of their intelligence. One Monday morning in 2007 an article in the US technology magazine *Wired* opened with the statement: 'If the existential malaise of yet another Monday hasn't already got you down, here's something more: chimpanzees are probably better than you at math' (Keim, 3 December 2007).

A study conducted by Tetsuro Matsuzawa and colleagues at Kyoto University had found that one chimpanzee, Ayumu, was able to beat college students in a game where they had to touch empty squares on a computer screen in the same order as the numbers that had just been flashed on the screen. In the scientific journal *Current Biology*, the researchers reported that 'the chimpanzee subjects can memorize at a glance the Arabic numerals scattered on the touch screen monitor and Ayumu outperformed all of the human subjects both in speed and accuracy' (Inoue & Matsuzawa, 2007). When the numerals remained on-screen for four-fifths of a second, the college students performed on a par with Ayumu – the star performer

– with a success rate of around 80 percent. But when the numbers flashed up for just over one-fifth of a second, the students' success rate fell to below 30 percent, while Ayumu's remained around 80 percent.

BBC News claimed these findings suggest we may have 'under-estimated the intelligence of our closest living relatives'. The researchers themselves were more circumspect. At a press conference Matsuzawa explained that the chimps' memory abilities are reminiscent of 'eidetic imagery', a special ability to retain a detailed and accurate image of a complex scene or pattern. This 'photographic memory' is known to be present in some normal human children, and then the ability declines with age.

Eidetic memory is in fact an ability selected for through evolution which has nothing to do with intelligence. As Jeremy Taylor writes: 'Tiny children have this skill before it becomes engulfed by language and a genuine symbolic understanding of numerals' (Taylor, 2009: 11). This is something my husband discovered, much to his surprise, when being thrashed by a three- and a four-year-old child while playing the 'Memory Game' – where one has to memorise the location of cards turned upside-down and try to retrieve matching pairs.

The parallels drawn between apes and humans are far from new. On seeing an orang-utan in London's Regent Park Zoo in 1842, Queen Victoria was fascinated but repulsed, exclaiming: 'how frightful and painfully and disagreeably human'. But whatever first impressions might tell us, apes are really not 'just like us'. The fact that we share more than 98 percent of our genes with chimps does not necessarily tell us that much. We also share 60 to 70 percent of our DNA with goldfish and 50 percent with bananas. It would be rather meaningless to argue that we are 50 percent banana-like or that goldfish are two-thirds human.

In fact, there are a number of scientists who argue that the genetic gap between humans and chimpanzees is far larger than molecular biology first indicated. In *Not a Chimp*, Jeremy Taylor challenges 'the basis of a forty-year-old concept of human genetic chimp proximity' (Taylor, 2009: 147). Taylor does admit that 'over very appreciable lengths of their respective genomes, humans and chimpanzees are very similar indeed'. He writes: 'Despite 12 million years of evolutionary separation, 6 million for each species since the split from the common ancestor, we are surprisingly similar in our genes' (Taylor, 2009: 70).

But Taylor argues that despite the very small difference in the gene coding sequence between humans and chimps, scientists have discovered that some of the important differences are in the regulation of gene expression. So a small change can make an immense difference: the genetic difference between us and chimps may be much greater than the 98.8 percent figure implies, as our uniqueness is based on a powerful network of gene regulation, he argues.

Our genetic relatedness to the great apes therefore does not necessarily tell us much about what it means to be human. Steve Sailer (1999) writes in the US magazine *National Review*:

> [T]he oft-cited 98 percent figure for shared DNA is less impressive than it looks. Most DNA is unused, so natural selection never changes it. Another big chunk of your personal DNA controls the basics of earthly carbon-based life, and is extremely common across multitudinous organisms. Thus, one study found we share 70 percent of our DNA with yeast! Perhaps if you don't have a great ape around, you can scrape by letting a packet of Fleischmann's Quick-Rise pinch-hit as your role model.

It is sloppy simply to apply human characteristics and motives to animals. It not only denigrates what is unique about our humanity, but also blocks our understanding of animal behaviour. Stephen Budiansky's fascinating book *If A Lion Could Talk* shows instead how evolutionary ecology (the study of how natural selection has equipped animals to lead the lives they do) has given us great insights into how animals process information in ways that are unique to them (Budiansky, 1998).

Budiansky notes that animals do incredibly stupid things in situations very similar to those where they previously seemed to show some degree of intelligence. In one of the first textbooks of comparative psychology (1894), the British experimental psychologist Conway Lloyd Morgan showed how the seemingly intelligent behaviours of some animals are most often better explained by chance. While taking two Scottish terriers for a walk with a friend - each dog carrying a light cane in its mouth – Morgan was amused to witness the dogs' daft attempts to negotiate their way through a narrow gate. Both dogs got stuck when their sticks repeatedly smashed against the gate's posts. Morgan wrote:

> There was a little scrimmaging, and some further ineffectual struggles, and then both dropped the sticks and came through. Their master sent them back to 'fetch'. The first to arrive at the gap just put his head through, seized a cane by the end and dragged it after him (Morgan, 1903: 254).

Had the story ended there one would be forgiven for believing that this terrier had thought about the problem – after its initial rather stupid attempt to get the stick through the gate – and come up with a better solution. That is, the dog may have worked out that dragging the cane by its end rather than carry it in the middle would do the trick. As Morgan noted: 'if the observations had been carried no further, one might have supposed that he clearly perceived the best means to effect the desired result' (Morgan, 1903: 255). However when they got back to the gate on their return journey both dogs surprisingly tried to smash their way through the gate while carrying their sticks in the middle – getting nowhere, of course. The initial seemingly intelligent behaviour of one of the terriers was clearly the result of chance, not any kind of insight.

The reason animals will do seemingly intelligent things one minute and incredibly stupid things the next minute is because they lack any conscious awareness of what they are doing. They are not able to contemplate the best course of action before acting, or to reflect on what they have done afterwards. Instead much of their behaviour can be explained on the basis of what the world-famous behaviourist B F Skinner called 'associative learning' (Skinner, 1974). This is a kind of trial and error learning, where certain actions are repeated if they have been positively rewarded and other actions are avoided if the results have been unfavourable.

Building on the work of the Nobel prize-winning physician Ivan Pavlov – who famously conditioned dogs to salivate in response to the sound of a ringing bell – Skinner claimed that all learning was the result of this kind of association between an action and a reinforcer. He was way off the mark trying to explain all human learning on the basis of positive and negative reinforcement, but this simple rule of conditioning has helped us understand much of animals' behaviour. Animals behave the way they do because particular behaviours have had certain consequences in the past, not because they have any insight into why they are doing what they are doing.

But not all animals learn from the same types of associations. Instead, many animals are 'hard-wired' to learn in very particular ways: their learning is highly specialised, with the types of associations they learn from differing from species to species. So, for instance, cats learn from pawing at things in their environment and pigeons learn from pecking at things.

Many will marvel at a cat's ability to open a closed door – claiming that this surely shows some degree of intelligence. However an interesting experiment carried out in the early twentieth century by the psychologist Edward Thorndike showed that when cats were placed in a 'puzzle box' where they had to push levers or pull strings to escape, their success was clearly the result of random pawing – not insight (Thorndike, 1911). By chance, after several minutes of pawing, scratching and biting, cats would perform an action that freed them from the box. Thorndike found that once the cats succeeded in pushing the right levers or pulling the right strings, they quickly learned from this association. They were then able to repeat the successful action again and again. However if the flap was opened only when the cats licked or scratched themselves it took the cats a lot longer to learn from this association.

Pigeons, on the other hand, learn from pecking. BF Skinner spent hours painstakingly training pigeons to perform all kinds of amusing and amazing feats, such as playing ping pong or performing short tunes on a toy piano (Skinner, 1951; 1974). He was able to train them to do so by rewarding them with food whenever they pecked particular objects. The pigeons quickly repeated those behaviours that resulted in a reward. Skinner would then keep fine-tuning their behaviour – for instance by only rewarding the pigeon if it pecked the object in a particular order or direction – until he had achieved his desired result.

The reason pigeons can learn to play ping-pong or perform a tune on a piano is because they are adept at learning from the association between pecking something and gaining a reward. Pigeons can also be trained to flap their wings in a particular way to avoid an electric shock. But it is almost impossible to teach them to peck a particular key in order to avoid an electric shock, or to flap their wings in order to get food (Foree & Lolordo, 1973). This is because the associations they learn from with ease are related to natural responses that have evolved for their species: pigeons naturally peck at things to get food and naturally flap their wings to flee from danger. They do not naturally peck at things to avoid danger or flap their wings to get food.

A famous experiment by the psychologists John Garcia and Robert Koelling on taste aversion in rats similarly shows the restricted nature of animal learning (Garcia & Koelling, 1966). They investigated the effect on rats of pairing a particular taste with either nausea or an electric shock. The rats avoided a novel taste if it was followed by nausea, even if the illness occurred several hours later. But they did not learn to avoid a novel taste when it was followed by an electric shock. Rats are particularly prone to associate nausea with the last thing they consumed, which – in evolutionary terms – would give a survival advantage to a forager that feeds on so many different kinds of food resources. But it is unlikely that there would have been any events in rats' evolutionary past that would have given them a survival advantage if they were able to learn from the association of a particular taste with a sudden trauma, such as an electric shock.

This shows that animals learn from certain associations depending on how they have evolved. As the evolutionary psychologist Richard Byrne writes in *The Thinking Ape: Evolutionary origins of intelligence*: 'Learning and genetic predispositions are intricately meshed in an animal's development' (Byrne, 2006: 37). American psychologist Martin Seligman described this phenomenon as 'preparedness': animals are prepared by their genetic make-up to learn from certain associations and only with great difficulty or not at all from other associations. As Budiansky similarly argues, non-human animal brains are wired by 'ecological adaptations' that are specific to their species. Because of a chance mutation and recombination of genes – in the distant past – cats, for instance, were endowed with the ability to learn from pawing at things in their environment, and rats were endowed with the ability to learn to avoid noxious foods. Their clever feats are not the result of any kind of insight.

An example that has caused much irritation to those who argue that animals do indeed have minds and possess human-like intelligence and insight is that of the stallion Clever Hans. The leading behavioural ecologist Donald Griffin, author of *Animal Minds: Beyond cognition to consciousness*, has complained that any evidence of animals being consciously aware 'routinely elicits a sort of knee-jerk accusation that they result from Clever Hans errors' (Griffin, 2001: 29).

Clever Hans was a horse that belonged to a retired schoolmaster, Wilhelm von Osten, a century ago. Osten was a devoted owner who spent hour upon hour educating his horse in order to prove that animals are as intelligent as human beings. He first taught Clever Hans to recognise numbers, and, at length, moved on to fairly complex calculations, including multiplications and divisions. Clever Hans would tap out the answer with his hoof and was rewarded with a sugar cube whenever he got it right. Scientists around the world were astounded, but they could not find any evidence of trickery.

Clever Hans rapidly became world famous. But some scientists remained sceptical and set out to test whether there may have been an alternative explanation for the horse's success. One of the scientists, a German psychologist named Oskar Pfungst, suggested testing whether the horse could work out the right answer if no other person in the room knew what calculation had been presented on the blackboard. As he predicted, Clever Hans was not so clever after all, and failed every one of those tests. It transpired that what the horse had done was watch the person who presented the mathematical challenge – rather than what was written on the board – and had picked up on inadvertent cues given by the questioner once Clever Hans had made the right number of taps, such as specific facial expressions or subtle bodily movements.

Donald Griffin bemoans the incessant references in the literature on animal behaviour to the danger of 'Clever Hans errors'. 'The saga of Clever Hans has been almost universally accepted by scientists as a definitive example of mistaken inference of complex mental abilities in animals', he writes (Griffin, 2001: 30). This may be true. But maybe the reason Clever Hans is referred to so often is precisely because it is one of the rare pieces of 'evidence' of animals having the ability to manipulate abstract symbols.

It is of course remarkable that horses can pick up on such subtle cues – that is, cues that weren't apparent to any human being until the actions of those people in Clever Hans' presence were carefully analysed. But this has nothing to do with conscious insight. As Budiansky explains: 'Horses, as social, herd-dwelling animals adapted to an open environment, have a remarkable evolved ability to pick up on subtle visual cues from their fellows' (Budiansky, 1998: xxxi).

In the entertaining TV programme *The Dog Whisperer*, César Millán shows how important it is to understand and to treat dogs *as dogs*, and not to read human emotions and human motivations into their behaviour. The César Millán website states:

> In the wild, a dog's very survival depends on a strong, stable, and organized pack, where every member knows its place and follows the rules established by the pack leader. The pack instinct is perhaps the strongest natural motivator for a dog.

By training dog-owners to behave more like pack leaders, César is able to help them get rid of the dogs' unwanted and sometimes aggressive behaviours.

During the programme César demonstrates again and again the extent to which the dogs are influenced by their owners' emotions. Any sense of foreboding or insecurity on the part of the owner – or any other human in their midst – is picked up on immediately by the dogs. Does this mean that the dogs are good psychologists with a sophisticated empathetic understanding of human feelings? Of course not.

They are merely acting like dogs – that is, following their dog instincts.

It is often claimed that dogs can 'smell fear'. Although they don't literally smell fear, there is a lot of truth in this assertion. Dogs sense quickly if someone in close proximity to them is alarmed. They pick up on this in several ways: visually, by observing hesitation in movement; aurally, by detecting a speeding up of heartbeat (which dogs can hear from up to five feet away); and by olfactory means, smelling various stress hormones.

Therefore, if a person who fears dogs runs away when spotting a dog, that dog will most likely run after them. It will do so because it has sensed the person's fear and believes that it too needs to run away from some non-specific danger. The dog will not know whether it is the person it is running after that it should fear or whether it is something else completely.

The dog's behaviour is not the result of any insight into the situation it is faced with - it does not think 'Here's a frightened person I can terrorise by chasing them' in the cowardly way a school bully will pick on the person they sense is most scared of them. Instead the dog is acting instinctively. This ability to sense fear – acquired from a chance mutation in dogs' distant evolutionary past – would have given dogs an important survival advantage. By being able to pick up on another's fear so quickly the dog's ancestors would have been alerted immediately to any danger, and by running after the conspecific (an animal of the same species) that showed fear, they would have had a better chance of escaping that potential threat.

An understanding of an animal's evolutionary past can therefore explain a lot about why it behaves the way it does. When it comes to human beings, however, our evolutionary past tells us very little about why we behave the way we do today. This is because we have something no other animal has: human consciousness, the ability to think about a problem before approaching it, reflect on what we are doing while we are doing it and refine our actions accordingly. We are the only species that is not constrained by our biology. Our biology is the precondition for our humanity, but our instincts are transformed into something very different as a result of human consciousness and culture.

As I explore in later chapters, it may possibly be the case that the great apes do possess some rudimentary form of human-like insight. But the limitations of this rudimentary insight (if it exists at all) become clear when exploring the emergence of insight in young children. Recently the Australian digital media site *NEWS.com.au* reported:

> In another case of researchers reporting the bleeding obvious, European scientists have found that children are smarter than chimpanzees (News.com.au, 2007).

Researchers at the Max Planck Institute for Evolutionary Anthropology in Leipzig in Germany gave a battery of tests to 105 human two-year-olds, 106 chimpanzees and 32 orang-utans and found that the children were far more advanced than the apes in social cognition tests (Herrmann *et al.*, 2007). 'Social cognition skills are critical for learning,' said Esther Herrmann, lead author of the research paper published in the journal *Science*, adding:

> The children were much better than the apes in understanding nonverbal communications, imitating another's solution to a problem and understanding the intentions of others (American Association for the Advancement of Science, 2007).

Swiss developmental psychologist Jean Piaget illustrated clearly the transformation that takes place in children's thinking, and therefore also their problem-solving abilities, from the latter part of their second year (Piaget, 1952). Children under 18 months of age, just like apes and other animals, solve problems mainly by trial and error. That is, when faced with a problem they need to solve without help from an adult, they do not make use of mental representations or 'symbolic thinking', as Piaget named it, in order to carry out tasks. However by the end of their second year of life toddlers do show evidence of being able to find solutions to problems just by *thinking* about them: they acquire the ability to invent new approaches to problems by working with mental images of potential solutions. In other words, they make predictions. They experiment with objects and problems in their mind before putting their plan into action.

As I show in later chapters, the differences in language, tool-use, self-awareness and insight between apes and humans are vast. A human child, even as young as two years of age, is intellectually head and shoulders above any ape. However, the question of whether apes have the *rudiments* of our unique human abilities – abilities that have allowed us to develop language, build cities, create great art and literature and much more – is an interesting one. An exploration of the extent to which apes resemble us may give us some insight into the evolutionary origins of human capabilities, but it will also show us how great the differences are between apes and humans.

In 2005, I met one of the world's foremost primatologists, Frans de Waal, to discuss his forthcoming book *Our Inner Ape: The past and future of human nature*. He suggested my approach to these questions was completely wrong: 'You are talking about the unique capacities of humans', he mocked, 'but genetically we are 98.5 per cent identical to chimps and bonobos, and mentally, socially and emotionally we are probably also 98.5 percent identical to chimps and bonobos. We love to emphasise that little difference that exists and cling to it and make a big deal out of it, but the similarities vastly outnumber the differences.'

In *Just Another Ape?* I am indeed 'making a big deal' out of the differences between humans and apes. One needs to go beyond first impressions and anecdotal evidence in order to establish the differences, and the alleged similarities, between human beings and the great apes. The fact is that the evidence for apes having human-like mental capacities is weak, and getting weaker as researchers develop more sophisticated ways of investigating what apes can and cannot do.

Chapter Two

Tool-use and Tool-making: Do Primates Have 'Culture'?

'As the soil, however rich it may be, cannot be productive without cultivation, so the mind without culture can never produce good fruit.'

Lucius Annaeus Seneca, (4 BC–65 AD).

The parting words of Frans de Waal, after we had discussed his forthcoming book *Our Inner Ape*, were: 'I hope you don't portray me as pessimistic.' De Waal wanted to stress that his idea of human and ape equivalence was not at all fatalistic. In the book he argues that 'peaceful by nature, [bonobos] belie the notion that ours is a purely bloodthirsty lineage': 'Bonobos make love, not war. They're the hippies of the primate world.'

He told me:

To have two close relations with strikingly different societies is extraordinarily instructive. The power-hungry and brutal chimp contrasts with the peace-loving and erotic bonobo – a kind of Dr Jekyll and Mr Hyde. Our own nature is an uneasy marriage of the two.

De Waal believes we should take some comfort from the fact that humans are not naturally *all* bad.

A couple of years earlier, in May 2002, when Francis Fukuyama was in Britain promoting his book *Our Posthuman Future*, we met to discuss his thesis on the future of humanity. I was left with the sense that the future according to Fukuyama was quite bleak, but his defence of human uniqueness was refreshing. He told me that human superiority is 'not necessarily an ignorant and self-serving prejudice on the part of human beings, but a belief about human dignity'. In *Our Posthuman Future*, Fukuyama writes: 'Human beings are free to shape their own behaviour because they are cultural animals capable of self-modification.'

The idea that human beings are the architects of our own destiny is not new. As Karl Marx famously wrote: 'Men make their own history, but not in circumstances of their own choosing'. As human beings we are capable of shaping our own future, while things just happen to animals.

This history-making potential – and with that an ability to improve our conditions – has been made possible through our ability to reflect on what we, and our fellow human beings, are doing – thereby teaching, and learning from, each other. We not only learn from human beings we come into direct contact with, but from people who lived and died long before we were born. This generation-upon-generation growth in human capacities has, for a long time, been seen as our defining characteristic.

But questions are now being raised as to whether we really are unique in being 'cultural animals' capable of self-modification. The idea that the great apes are 'just like us' is becoming increasingly popular. But if apes did share our ability for self-modification, would we not see some evidence of this in the way they live their lives in the wild? If they possessed something as powerful as self-conscious awareness and the ability to co-operate and learn from each other, would they not have used it to move beyond their hand-to-mouth existence in the way human beings have?

When I put this to Frans de Waal, his response was that: 'If we consider the issue of the accumulation of knowledge there are parallels between humans and the great apes'. I had visions of apes reading books, composing music or teaching algebra, but that's not what was being suggested.

Instead when de Waal talked about 'the accumulation of knowledge' he was referring to apes acquiring and passing on skills such as how to use sticks to fish for termites or stones to crack nuts.

Even the most enthusiastic proponent of ape rights would have to admit that these skills have not led to any significant changes in the way apes live their lives. Human societies, on the other hand, have become ever more complex. In his 1876 pamphlet *The Part Played by Labour in the Transition from Ape to Man*, Karl Marx's collaborator Friedrich Engels argued that each generation has been able to build on the abilities of previous generations, with the work of each generation becoming 'different, more perfect and more diversified.' He wrote: 'Agriculture was added to hunting and cattle raising; then came spinning, weaving, metalworking, pottery and navigation. Along with trade and industry, art and science finally appeared' (Engels, 1982: 10). And as cognitive archaeologist Steven Mithen argues in *The Prehistory of the Mind*, since the birth of agriculture around ten thousand years ago, events have flashed past at bewildering speed: 'People create towns and then cities. [I]n no more than an instant carts have become cars and writing tablets word processors', he writes (Mithen, 1998: 21).

A few hundred years ago it would have taken several days to get a message from London to Edinburgh. But ever since Samuel Morse transmitted his famous telegraph 'What hath God wrought?' from Washington to Baltimore in 1844, the means by which we can communicate with each other – over short and long distances – have not only been revolutionised but have become ubiquitous. We can communicate instantaneously with others almost anywhere in the world, and we can get from one side of the globe to another in less time than it took people in the middle ages to get from London to Edinburgh. Our lives have changed much more in just the past decade – in terms of the technology we use, how we communicate with each other, and how we form and sustain personal relationships – than the lives of apes have over millions of years.

Cultural critic Angus Kennedy writes on *spiked*:

The world has become more civilised over the past 50 years than anything in the popular imagination allows credit for. Whether it is 300 million people lifted from poverty in China – almost equivalent to the entire population of the United States – or continuing advances in living standards, literacy, information technology and life expectancy, civilisation has been everywhere on the march (Kennedy, 2009).

Undoubtedly, whatever 'cultural' capabilities apes do have they are a lot less powerful than those human beings possess: there is minimal evidence of them using any such capacities in the wild. But it may be the case that they do have something resembling human culture in its embryonic form – something far less powerful than human cultural transmission, but something that can give us an insight into the evolutionary emergence of our unique abilities.

Some argue that regional variations in animal tool-use show that it is not simply instinctive, but passed on 'culturally'. In an extensive review of existing field studies of chimpanzee behaviour, the evolutionary and developmental psychologist Andrew Whiten and his colleagues concluded that there are at least 39 local variations in the apes' behavioural patterns (Whiten *et al.*, 1999). That is, there are particular types of tool-use, foraging techniques, communication and grooming rituals that are common in some chimp groups and absent in others. A similar review led by the Dutch primatologist Carel van Schaik found 19 local variations among groups of orang-utans (van Schaik *et al.*, 2003). The researchers concluded that in the 39 cases of 'local traditions' amongst chimps and the 19 cases amongst orang-utans, alternative genetic (or, in other words evolutionary) explanations or ecological explanations (for instance, the presence of certain nuts in some environments and not others) were improbable, and that the local variations indicated instead that the apes were capable of learning new skills and – most importantly – passing them on to their fellows.

Steven Mithen recognises that much has been made of Whiten's finding. He writes:

This finding has been like a blast of trumpets for those who have wanted to minimise the differences between chimpanzee and human behaviour. For it seems to say that chimpanzees are like humans: animals with culture (1998: 83).

For instance, in the *African Journal of Ecology* Jon Lovett and Andrew Marshall from the Centre for Ecology, Law and Policy at the University of York, argue that nonhuman primates deserve special status, not only because 'they are genetically and behaviourally similar to humans', but because 'chimpanzees have been shown to possess distinctive community behaviour patterns that can be described as cultures' (Lovett & Marshall, 2006: 1).

But does it? How do we explain the discovery of 'cultural traditions' among chimps and orang-utans? The key question is whether these regional variations can be explained by 'cultural transmission' – where new skills are passed on to the next generation through some kind of social learning - rather than merely through genetics, ecological variations or chance.

The first evidence of what could be interpreted as cultural transmission among primates was found in the 1950s in Japan among macaque monkeys. One juvenile female, named Imo, began washing sand off sweet potatoes provided by researchers. Later her mother and closest peers were observed doing the same. Within a decade, the whole of the population under middle age was washing potatoes.

The question that needed to be answered was whether these behaviours had spread due to some form of social learning such as imitation and possibly even teaching. Until recently being able to imitate, or 'ape', was not seen as particularly clever. As Richard Byrne, writes in *The Thinking Ape: Evolutionary origins of intelligence*:

> [A]nimal imitation used to be dismissed: a cheap trick that animals often use, which produces a spurious mimicry of real intelligence. From this lowly status imitation has recently been promoted to a sign of remarkable intellectual ability, one which involves a symbolic process [...]. And ironically it is *now* suggested that imitation can only be done by humans (Byrne, 2006: 54).

Indeed, imitation properly understood involves being able to appreciate not just what an act looks like when performed by another individual, but also what it is like to do that act oneself. One must be able to put oneself in another person's shoes, so to speak. If apes, and maybe even other primates, were found to be capable of aping, then, it would imply that they are capable of quite complex cognitive processes.

The fact that there are local variations in behavioural patterns among primates could indicate that they are learning through imitation. But this is not necessarily the case. It has become apparent that the spread of particular behavioural patterns – such as potato washing among macaque monkeys – may well happen by other means.

Comparative psychologist Bennett Galef scrutinised the data from Japan and found that the rate at which the behaviour spread among the monkeys was very slow and steady, not accelerating as one might expect in the case of imitation (Galef, 1992). After all, the beauty of imitation is that each individual who adopts a new behaviour then serves as a model for others, so the behaviour can spread rapidly. But after Imo had discovered how to wash the sand off the potatoes, it took up to a decade for the tiny group of monkeys to acquire the habit. Galef argued that the potato washing was either inadvertently encouraged by the caretakers or it was discovered by chance by each of the macaques that took it up, but it wasn't the result of imitation.

Reviewing the literature on primate behaviour, it emerges that there is in fact no consensus among scientists as to whether any primates – even the great apes – are capable of imitation (Tennie *et al.*, 2009; Whiten, 2000; Whiten *et al.*, 2009). Instead it could be the case that the differences in their behavioural repertoires are the result of what has been termed *stimulus enhancement* or *emulation*.

Stimulus enhancement is when an animal is drawn to, and more likely to approach, something in their environment because another member of their species is interacting with it. It is an effective way of learning, because once they are drawn to the particular stimulus the chance of them learning the new skill by trial and error is greatly increased. As Richard Byrne writes: 'Stimulus enhancement would enable much more efficient learning, so it is just the sort of simple rule that we might have expected natural selection to have equipped social animals with' (Byrne, 2006: 57). The underlying mechanism is still trial and error learning, or conditioning, rather than any insight or a capacity in animals to put themselves in the shoes of another.

For instance, it has been shown that birds are more attracted to a particular feeding site if they see another bird finding food there. In other words, the bird's attention has been drawn to the stimulus, but this does not necessarily imply any knowledge or appreciation of the significance of the particular stimulus. Birds do not make a calculation that they too will find food at the site: they go there instinctively. Take the spread of the habit among various species of small birds of peeling off the foil from milk bottles in order to drink the thick cream covering the milk inside. This behaviour was found to spread gradually throughout England in the 1930s and was for a long time attributed to imitation (Fisher and Hinde, 1949). But as Donald Griffin admits:

> The basic motion used by tits to open milk bottles were much the same as those used to pull layers of bark from vegetation. This has led many to feel that birds' discovery that milk bottles were a source of food was not so novel after all because it did not require the development of a whole new motor pattern (Griffin, 2001: 53).

When tested, the claim that birds are capable of imitation was found wanting. In a laboratory setting, those birds that were given the opportunity to watch another bird opening a milk bottle in an adjacent cage were no more likely to learn how to open the milk bottle in their cage than those that had a view of a bird without a milk bottle (Sherry and Galef, 1984). So when their attention was drawn to the milk bottle – by placing it in their cage – it did not help the birds at all to be able to see another bird pulling the foil off the top of a milk bottle. They simply happened on the technique themselves, or not.

Another explanation for the spread of particular be-havioural patterns is *emulation,* a concept first developed by the psychologist David Wood. *Emulation* is when the result of another person or animal's behaviour is reproduced, rather than the method for achieving it. Wood wrote that 'children not only attempt to impersonate others by imitating their actions but also try to emulate them by achieving similar ends or objectives' (Wood, 1989: 71). He found 'instances where children achieve common goals to those modelled, but do so by using idiosyncratic means that were never observed' (Wood 1989: 72). He pointed out that – with emulation – the copiers strive to achieve the same end-result as the model they are copying. They may happen purely by chance to find the same method as the model, which, as Whiten and colleagues point out, 'might thus be falsely recorded as imitation' (Whiten *et al.*, 2009: 2419).

Thus, superficially emulation may look like imitation, but the way emulation works is that, after having watched someone else carry out a task with a particular tool, a person or animal merely learns that the tool can be used to obtain rewards. With *imitation*, on the other hand, the person or animal learns *how* the tool can be manipulated to obtain the reward. Neither emulation or imitation should be confused with *mimicry*, which refers to the instinctive reproduction of certain behaviours with no understanding of the demonstrator's intention – such as a new-born baby mimicking another's tongue protrusion or parrots mimicking human speech. Mimicry involves copying body movements or acts that were part of the mimicker's motor repertoire before they were mimicked.

Recent experiments have indicated that apes have the ability to emulate rather than to imitate. Unlike humans, who show great flexibility in how they imitate – being able to focus on the sequence of bodily actions used to achieve an outcome, or on the outcome itself, or, indeed, on the goal or intention of the demonstrator, chimps seem only to focus on the outcome of a demonstration. Post-doctoral researcher, Claudio Tennie, with Josep Call and Michael Tomasello, at the Max Planck Institute for Evolutionary Anthropology, found that four-year-old children could learn through imitation to fold a piece of string into a loop – in effect making a lasso – and pull an out-of-reach block containing a reward towards them (Tennie *et al.*, 2009). None of the apes – seven chimpanzees, six gorillas, eight orang-utans and five bonobos – were able to copy the demonstrator and make such a loop in order to retrieve a reward.

An earlier study by Tomasello and colleagues (1987) was key in showing that apes can emulate but not imitate. The researchers showed one group of chimpanzees a human using a T-bar to rake in out-of-reach food. The other group of chimpanzees also saw the human but were given no demonstration of how to use the T-bar. They found that those apes that had seen the model using the T-bar as a rake were more likely to use the tool for a similar purpose. But 'none of the subjects demonstrated an ability to imitatively copy the demonstrator's precise behavioural strategies', Tomasello and colleagues write (Tomasello *et al.*, 1987: 175). They argue that the apes used emulation rather than the more simple form of social learning, stimulus enhancement, since while both groups manipulated the T-bar, only the chimps who had seen it being used as a tool used it as a tool themselves.

Tennie and colleagues persuasively argue that because apes are only able to focus on the outcome – rather than the sequence of steps that make up the action – they are not able to learn as humans do. They write: 'Behaviours one sees as part of chimpanzee culture are all things that individual chimpanzees could invent on their own fairly readily if all of the external and internal conditions are right' (Tennie *et al.*, 2009: 2408). Once a member of the species has invented a novel behaviour, it becomes more likely that other members of the group will repeat this behaviour – 'and this they do basically on their own by mostly re-inventing it', or in other words, by emulating what their fellows have done. The chimps 're-construct the product rather than copy the process leading to it' and therefore they 'have to "re-invent the wheel" at each transmission step' (Tennie *et al.*, 2009: 2407). What this means is that nonhuman ape cultures are 'restricted by the upper boundaries of their species physical cognitive skills'.

The fact that it takes chimps up to four years to acquire the necessary skills to select and adequately use tools to crack nuts implies that they are not capable of true imitation, and definitely not teaching (Mithen, 1998). Young chimps invest a lot of time and effort in attempts to crack nuts that are, after all, an important part of their diet. The slow rate of their development raises serious questions about their ability to reflect on what their fellow apes are doing and copy the steps involved in cracking nuts.

Humans clearly have a higher technical intelligence and are better innovators than apes, but this alone cannot explain the vast gap between ape and human abilities. No human being on their own could invent from scratch a bicycle, never mind anything as complex as a television or a mobile phone. Yet hundreds of thousands of people world-wide – people who may indeed be quite clever but are by no means geniuses – are at any one moment involved in the invention of ever-more sophisticated appliances, means of communication, medicines, and much more.

The reason human beings are capable of such clever feats is because we are able *both* to learn through imitation and teaching, that is to learn from others' intelligent innovations, *and* to solve problems through innovation – that is, discovering novel solutions, either on our own or through collaboration. This leads to a generation-upon-generation accumulation of knowledge, discoveries and innovations.

'This accumulation is presumably due, or at least plausibly due, to some unique processes of social learning and transmission', the Max Planck Institute for Evolutionary Anthropology team argue (Tennie *et al.*, 2009: 2407). We, in some instances, rely on emulation learning – like apes and other animals – but we are also able to pay attention to others' behaviours and strategies, and therefore can copy what they do with a high degree of fidelity.

It is this ability to learn from others and 'participate in a collective cognition' that sets us apart from all other species, Tomasello argues. He writes:

> [S]uch social gifts make all the difference. Imagine a child born alone on a desert island and somehow magically kept alive. What would this child's cognitive skills look like as an adult – with no one to teach her, no one to imitate, no pre-existing tools, no spoken or written language? She would certainly possess basic skills for dealing with the physical world, but they would not be particularly impressive. She would not invent for

herself English, or Arabic numerals, or metal knives, or money. These are the products of collective cognition; they were created by human beings, in effect, putting their heads together. It is because they are adapted for such cultural activities — and not because of their cleverness as individuals — that human beings are able to do so many exceptionally complex and impressive things (Tomasello, 25 May 2008).

It is this unique ability to copy complex actions and strategies (even those that the individual doing the copying would never have been able to come up with on their own), along with unique forms of co-operation and an ability to teach, that create the uniquely powerful 'ratchet effect' in human culture, whereby gains are consolidated and built on rather than having to be rediscovered.

Intriguingly, the other great apes — bonobos, gorillas and orang-utans — have not been found to use tools for different purposes in the wild. It is only chimps that do so. In captivity, however, all the great apes have used and perfected tools, and there is even evidence that they may have some understanding of how tools work, or, some ability to form mental representations of what a tool should be like. In captivity they may also show some evidence of social learning, such as imitation.

For instance, Andrew Whiten and colleagues set out to investigate the extent of the 'cultural capacities' of apes by conducting large-scale, controlled experiments with captive chimpanzees (Whiten *et al.*, 2007). As the researchers point out, field experiments often rely on circumstantial inference about whether social learning is or is not taking place, while experimental studies are sometimes able to answer questions that field studies cannot answer with any degree of certainty.

The researchers separately presented six groups of between eight and eleven chimpanzees with two tool-use problems — both involving the extraction of food from a container and each solvable by two different techniques.

In the absence of instruction, none of the chimpanzees managed to extract any of the food. Two chimps from separate groups were then taken aside and trained to extract the food — one chimp being taught to use a lifting techniques (lifting an obstacle so that the trapped food was released) and the other group being taught an alternative poking technique (inserting the tool into an obscured opening to push the obstacle out of the way). Within minutes of these chimps returning to their compounds other individuals successfully learned how to solve the tasks. The fact that most chimpanzees learned to extract the food within hours, and in some cases minutes, indicates that chimps were at least capable of *emulation*. The fact that the chimps tended to use the technique that they had witnessed, rather than the alternative equally effective technique, *could* indicate that they were indeed capable of *imitation*.

The researchers concluded:

> ... chimpanzees have a demonstrable capacity for fidelity in social learning across multiple groups, consistent with the hypothesis that regional behaviour patterns in Africa have spread through cultural transmission' (Whiten *et al.*, 2007: 2).

But the Max Planck Institute for Evolutionary Anthropology team argue that 'the apes did not learn anything radically new or improbable'. They did not learn anything that they would not be able to invent on their own. Instead they 'had their attention drawn to things by the demonstrators, and then solved the problem for themselves (Tennie *et al.*, 2009: 2407). Tennie and colleagues argue that nonhuman apes are only able to copy tasks that they 'could in principle learn for themselves' (Tennie *et al.*, 2009: 2408). Compare this to everyday human behaviours and ways of thinking – whether it be reading and writing, driving a car, or performing basic calculations when paying for goods – none of which we could have invented on our own if left to our own devises.

More recently Whiten has conceded that apes have nowhere near the same capacity to imitate as human children. In 2009 he told the *New Scientist* that children imitate each step of an action with far more fidelity than chimps, even when some of the steps are superfluous. 'We are such a cultural species that it pays children to copy everything that adults do,' he said (Callaway, 2009).

The limitation of ape abilities with regard to imitation is apparent in a more recent experiment carried out by Whiten and a colleague Sarah Marshall-Pescini (Marshall-Pescini & Whiten, 2008). Eleven young chimpanzees were presented with a foraging device for extracting honey. This device could be used in a simple way by 'dipping' it into a hole in a box to extract small amounts of honey. It could also be used in a more complex way by 'probing': if the device was moved around in the hole in the box it would release a latch that opened the box, giving the chimps access to all the honey. The probing technique incorporated the simple action of dipping but required further more complex actions, and was much more productive.

When a familiar human demonstrated how to use the device for dipping, five of the older chimps succeeded in extracting honey in that way. But none of the chimps adopted the more complex and productive probing technique when it was demonstrated to them. They seemed reluctant to adopt a more efficient technique if they already were able to use a technique that worked.

The researchers concluded that 'young chimpanzees exhibit a tendency to become "stuck" on a technique they initially learn, inhibiting cumulative social learning and possibly constraining the species' capacity for cumulative cultural evolution' (Marshall-Pescini & Whiten, 2008: 449). Having reviewed recent studies Whiten and colleagues found 'a remarkable consistency' in studies investigating the inflexibility of chimpanzees' social learning (Whiten *et al.*, 2009). 'What appears to be revealed is a social learning propensity [that] quickly becomes "canalized" or crystallised, producing a routine resistant to cumulative or other change', they write (Whiten *et al.*, 2009: 2426). This was not the case with human children: most three- and four-year olds jettisoned the simple, less efficient, strategy of 'dipping' for the more productive solution of 'probing' after seeing demonstrations of the technique. The reviewers conclude that 'since the human and chimpanzee lineages diverged, our species has acquired more refined capacities for both higher fidelity imitation and cumulative cultural learning' (Whiten *et al.*, 2009: 2427).

Whiten and colleagues argue that 'the evidence shows that both chimpanzees and children possess a "portfolio" of different social learning mechanisms, including both imitation and emulation, that are deployed selectively in different contexts' (Whiten *et al.*, 2009). The authors acknowledge 'considerable differences in the social learning propensities of the two species', but believe that 'we need to go beyond characterising the difference as a simple imitation/emulation dichotomy' (Whiten *et al.*, 2009).

But there is no conclusive evidence that apes in the wild are capable of even the simplest form of imitation. Indeed, in the literature on primate behaviour, most of the examples showing ape imitation come from situations where the apes have lived with humans – such as Viki the chimp and Chantek the orang-utan. Viki, raised by Keith and Catherine Hayes, was trained through an imitation game to reproduce various gestures when the experimenter said 'do this' (Hayes and Hayes, 1952). Instances of spontaneous imitation were also reported – such as operating a spray gun and opening the lid of a can with a screw-driver.

It could be the case that only chimpanzees with extensive human contact in early development acquire an, albeit limited, ability to imitate. In an experiment carried out by Michael Tomasello with primatologist Sue Savage-Rumbaugh and psychologist Ann Cale Kruger, the abilities of mother-reared chimpanzees, human-reared chimpanzees and 18-month-old human children were compared (Tomasello *et al.*, 1993). They found that the mother-reared chimpanzees were much poorer than the human-reared chimpanzees and the human children on a number of imitation tasks with different objects.

Melinda Carpenter and Josep Call, from the Max Planck Institute for Evolutionary Anthropology, have also demonstrated that 'encultured apes' – those raised by humans – do demonstrate different abilities from those 'reared by conspecifics' – that is, raised by fellow apes (Carpenter & Call, in press). Among mother-reared apes there is very little evidence of an ability to copy others' actions, they argue. As has already been argued, when apes attempt to reproduce results they are likely to do so using their own strategy. But Carpenter and Call also argue that even among the 'encultured apes' it is a challenge to faithfully imitate actions when told to 'do this': 'Apes do not do this spontaneously and it is laborious to train' (Carpenter and Call, in press: 18).

Revisiting the Hayes' experiment, comparative psychologist Deborah Custance and colleagues carried out a more rigorous follow-up study on two young human-reared chimpanzees', testing their ability to reproduce a number of gestures when told to 'do this' (Custance *et al.*, 1995). Only a third of the chimps' responses matched the gestures they were asked to copy. But even when the chimpanzees were able to copy the gestures of the human demonstrator, they were often not able to reproduce the actions exactly. For instance, if the demonstrator touched her nose with her index finger saying 'do this,' the chimps sometimes touched their noses but often with their middle fingers or thumbs. Most four-year-old human children are able to match such gestures perfectly (Whiten, 1996). When the human-reared orang-utan Chantek was trained to copy the actions and gestures of the caregiver when told to 'do this,' he showed a similar inability to replicate the detail of the movements demonstrated (Miles *et al.*, 1996).

Ironically then it does seem that apes are rather poor at aping – particularly those reared in the wild. As I have argued, imitation relies on an ability to think about what another being is doing, and to be able to put oneself in another person's shoes. Teaching – which is even more restricted among primates – relies on an ability to understand what another being does or does not know and understand. Richard Byrne concedes that only twice has intentional teaching of the young been convincingly recorded among chimpanzees, and never among other apes.

He writes:

> It remains unexplained why such an apparently valuable technique should be used so minimally by animals apparently capable of understanding its benefit. Either much teaching in great apes is being missed by observers, or teaching is not the great gift that our educational establishment believes it to be, or apes only partly understand their fellows' understanding and knowledge. The last alternative is perfectly possible, but, if

so, we have as yet no idea of where their deficiency lies (Byrne, 2006: 144–145).

The last possibility is the most likely. In fact, Michael Tomasello categorically argues that apes and monkeys 'do not intentionally teach other individuals new behaviours'. Furthermore, 'non-human primates do not point or gesture to outside objects for others; do not hold objects up to show them to others; [and,] do not actively offer objects to other individuals by holding them out' (Tomasello, 1999: 21).

He, and other colleagues at the Max Planck Institute for Evolutionary Anthropology, argue:

> Regardless of whether chimpanzee and human culture share some common mechanisms, which they almost certainly do, what is undeniable, we would claim, is that human culture is an evolutionarily unique phenomenon. *Prima facie* evidence of this uniqueness is the kind of products human cultures produce: material and symbolic artefacts from industrialized technologies to language, to money and to symbolic mathematics. These cultural products suggest the possibility of some unique types of cultural transmission processes in humans (Tennie *et al.*, 2009: 2405).

The differences between apes and humans are indeed vast. As Derek Penn and colleagues from the Cognitive Evolution Group at the University of Louisiana and the UCLA Reasoning Lab argue:

> Human animals – and no other – build fires and wheels, diagnose each other's illnesses, communicate using symbols, navigate with maps, risk their lives for ideals, collaborate with each other, explain the world in terms of hypothetical causes, punish strangers for breaking rules, imagine impossible scenarios, and teach each other how to do all of the above (Penn *et al.*, 2008).

To say that there is no substantial difference between cultural transmission among apes and humans is like saying there is no substantial difference between a glacier and a car – both move from A to B, albeit one a lot slower than the other. Six million years of ape evolution may have resulted in the emergence of

39 local behavioural patterns in tool-use, communication and grooming rituals. But this has not moved them beyond their hand-to-mouth existence.

Chapter Three
'Folk Physics': Do Apes Understand How Tools Work?

'Intelligence is not to make no mistakes, but quickly to see how to make them good.'

Bertolt Brecht, (1898–1956).

Michael Tomasello persuasively argues in his thought-provoking book *The Cultural Origins of Human Cognition* that cumulative cultural evolution depends on two processes – 'innovation and imitation (possibly supplemented by instruction)', and that it cannot be brought about by 'weaker' forms of social learning, such as stimulus enhancement or emulation (Tomasello, 1999: 39). Similarly, Andrew Whiten and Carel van Schaik argue that culture requires both innovation and social learning processes, where the latter must be 'powerful enough to turn innovations into traditions'. They add: 'Innovation is but one half of what is required for traditions and culture: the other half is social learning' (Whiten & van Schaik, 2007: 625).

Although some have argued that apes can innovate but not imitate, Steven Mithen (1998) argues that the reason ape tool-use does not progress from one generation to the next is because of an inability to imitate *and* an inability to innovate. He points out that we do not find cultural differences in human societies in the use of simple but essential tools: all human societies use knives, for instance. The fact that some chimp groups do not use sticks to fish for termites, rather than being evidence of cultural transmission, may instead indicate the limitations of their intelligence, Mithen argues. He writes:

> The failure of Tai Chimpanzees to use termite sticks is most likely to arise simply from the fact that no individual within the group has ever thought of doing such a thing, or discovered it accidentally, or managed to learn from another chimp before that chimp forgot how to do it, or passed away with his great tool-use secret. This is not cultural behaviour; it is simply not being very good at thinking about making and using physical objects. It is the absence of technical intelligence (Mithen, 1998: 83–84).

His argument is persuasive: particularly as primatologists have not found any technological advances in chimpanzee's tool-use over more than 40 years of observations in the wild. Instead 'each generation of chimpanzees appears to struggle to attain the technical level attained by the previous generation' (Mithen, 1998: 84).

Mithen concludes:

> Here is a summary of the evidence about tool-making and using by chimpanzees. Their tools are very simple. They are made by using physical actions common to other domains of behaviour. They are used for a limited range of tasks, and chimpanzees appear to be rather poor at thinking about new ways to use tools. They are slow at adopting the tool-use methods currently practised within their group (Mithen, 1998: 85)

Similarly Tomasello points out that if apes are not capable of imitation they are unlikely to acquire any novel, more effective techniques accidentally discovered by another ape. If they do not investigate *how* that ape is using the particular tool 'any other individuals watching [...] would use their own methods, and so the novel strategy would simply die out with the innovator', he writes (Tomasello 1999: 39).

In order to establish whether an animal's behaviour is the outcome of instinct combined with trial and error learning – and maybe a basic form of social learning such as stimulus enhancement or emulation – or whether it is the outcome of technical intelligence, it is far from sufficient to demonstrate the apparent sophistication of the tool-using and tool-making capacities of the animal in the wild.

A few years ago a *National Geographic* news item reported that a 'crafty' species of crow found on the Pacific islands of New Caledonia had been found not only to use tools, but even to develop and improve them (Pickrell, 2003). Zoologists from the University of Auckland had discovered that New Caledonian crows (*Corvus moneduloides*) were augmenting the insect-snagging tools they made from leaves. Lead researcher Gavin Hunt said: 'The ability to cumulatively improve tools is one of the features that define humanness. In fact this ability has been crucial for our technological progress. Our findings therefore remove an important technological difference between humans and other animals'(Pickrell, 2003). Hunt had been the first scientist to document that wild New Caledonian crows use a variety of different types of tools in order to obtain food, including straight sticks or leaf stems, hooked twigs or vines, and tools torn from the leaves of the Pandanus tree (Hunt, 1996; Hunt & Gray, 2004), but this new finding seemed even more impressive. So are these birds really 'intelligent'?

In Aesop's fable, a thirsty crow placed a pile of stones in a pitcher containing a small amount of water in order to raise the water level and reach it with its bill. Christopher Bird, zoologist at the University of Cambridge, and Nathan Emery, expert in corvid and primate cognition at Queen Mary University in London, recently designed an experiment to test whether four rooks could solve a problem analogous to that in Aesop's fable. They tested whether the rooks would raise the water level in a pitcher so that a floating worm moved into their reach. The researchers found that all four rooks solved the problem – even demonstrating an 'appreciation of precisely how many stones were needed' (Bird & Emery, 2009: 1410). Bird and Emery claim: 'New Caledonian crows appear to understand the functional properties of tools and solve complex physical problems via causal and analogical reasoning' (Bird & Emery, 2009: 1410).

The skills of other corvids (crows, rooks, jackdaws and jays) have been found to be equally impressive in laboratory settings. Zoologist Alex Weir and colleagues at the University of Oxford found that a female crow named Betty could spontaneously bend a piece of straight wire into a hook and successfully retrieve a bucket containing food from within an upright cylinder (Weir *et al.*, 2002). The researchers concluded:

> Our finding, in a species so distantly related to humans and lacking symbolic language, raises numerous questions about the kinds of understanding of 'folk physics' and causality available to nonhumans (Weir *et al.*, 2002: 981).

However, another group of zoologist at Oxford University who have studied the tool-use of New Caledonian crows for almost a decade – Lucas Bluff, Christian Rutz, Alex Kazelnik, Joanna Wimpenny and Christian Rutz – have warned that care needs to be taken when interpreting and describing results that seemingly imply that corvids have an understanding of "folk physics". 'Whilst it is now widely accepted that tool use *per se* is not indicative of unusual intelligence, the remarkable complexity of New Caledonian crows' natural [tool-oriented behaviour] has often led observers (lay people as well as scholars) to assume that this species may possess exceptionally advanced cognitive abilities', the zoologists point out (Bluff *et al*, 2007). But they conclude that the evidence for the birds having knowledge of the causal basis of tasks is murky. Instead the remarkable tool-use of New Caledonian crows may be another example of species-specific adaptations, they argue.

In an earlier paper, Kacelnik and colleagues illustrate the highly sophisticated web-making abilities of spiders, which even the keenest proponent of animal intelligence would find difficult to attribute to higher cognitive abilities:

> [In a tree], a spider moves between the branches and the ground, releasing various mixtures of liquid proteins with different proportions to form different kinds of silk on its trail. The spider's movements are such that the trail of silk forms a perfectly

designed web with a sticky spiral held by strong, non-sticky lines supporting the structure. This web building is achieved for an almost infinite variety of geometric configurations of the branches that provide potential support, thus creating a new solution to each problem. When the web is finished, the spider waits at its hub until an insect is trapped, when its own reward materialises (Kacelnik *et al.*, 2006).

The key issue here is that the spider's 'extremely sophisticated engineering achievements' does not necessarily tell us anything about an 'underlying cognitive complexity' (Kacelnik *et al.*, 2006). 'There are many examples of complex architecture – typically in the form of nests – throughout the animal kingdom, none of which are thought to require generally elevated cognitive abilities. Spiders have a complex, but rigid, built-in set of rules, shaped by evolution over many generations, and they respond to the spatial configuration of potential web supports with precisely pre-programmed behaviours', Kacelnik and colleagues write (Kacelnik *et al.*, 2006).

The flexibility of the New Caledonian crow's tool use indicates that we may need to look beyond 'precisely pre-programmed behaviours' as an explanation, Kacelnik and colleagues claim. They write:

> The behaviour of New Caledonian crows both in the wild and in captivity conveys the impression that these animals' cognitive capacities are out of the ordinary. Indeed, they fashion and select tools according to apparently pre-conceived projects, to an extent not reported so far in any other bird and hardly in any other animal. They show inventiveness in solving new problems with flexibility (Kacelnik *et al.*, 2006).

In his book *Not a Chimp*, Jeremy Taylor dedicates a chapter to the tool-making abilities of corvids, in order to illustrate that far too much has been made of the tool-using abilities of chimpanzees in the wild. Taylor shows that these birds equal, and in many cases better, anything observed with chimpanzees. 'In two species that parted company 280 million years ago, performance is either very similar, or corvids might even have an edge. Bird brains, in specific contexts, are a match for chimp brains', he writes.

Still, we do not necessarily need to turn to human-like intelligence as an explanation. It is true that flexible tool-use may indicate some degree of technical intelligence or insight. The Oxford University zoologists state that 'a fundamental feature of intelligence is flexibility: being able to alter one's behaviour if circumstances change'. To illustrate, they quote John Maynard Keynes, who famously replied to the criticism of having changed his position on monetary policy during the Great Depression that "When the facts change, I change my mind. What do you do, sir?"' (Bluff *et al.*, 2007).

However the laboratory experiments of Bluff and colleagues indicate that although the abilities of the crows are striking, 'they do not prove that this species is capable of understanding physical causality' (Bluff *et al*, 2007). The researchers concluded that the proficient tool oriented behaviours of the New Caledonian crows could result from 'a complex interplay of heritable predispositions, individual learning through object exploration, and (quite possibly) the acquisition of socially-transmitted information' (Bluff *et al.*, 2007). In other words, the crows' tool use could be the result of natural selection, combined with associative learning and a more simple form of social learning, such as stimulus enhancement.

The chimpanzee and the South American capuchin monkey are the only other animals found consistently to use tools for a number of different purposes in the wild. Capuchin monkeys use sticks for digging and for probing tree holes and rock crevices. They also use sticks for raking food, and as weapons to attack other monkeys and to kill snakes (Moura and Lee, 2004). Despite their tool-use being limited to sticks, the many different ways they use these tools could be taken as evidence of them having a cause and effect understanding of the properties of sticks as tools.

However pioneering work by the cognitive primatologist Elisabetta Visalberghi exposes the monkeys' lack of insight. She writes:

> Many years ago, while passing in front of a group of capuchin monkeys (*Cebus apella*) at the Rome Zoo, I was lucky to see an adult male pounding an unshelled peanut with a boiled potato. Why was he behaving like this? Peanuts can be opened easily and,

moreover, boiled potatoes are soft. […] The fact that capuchins were doing something smart in a silly way, or something silly in a smart way, struck my interest. […] What I have done since then is demonstrate, on the one hand, how successful capuchins are in solving problems and, on the other, how relatively little they understand of what they do (Visalberghi, 2004: 405).

Visalberghi designed an experiment demonstrating that capuchins can quickly learn how to use sticks to push nuts out of horizontal transparent tubes. The tubes were too long for the monkeys to be able to reach the nuts with their fingers and too narrow for their whole arm to fit in. But they had a number of sticks at their disposal. Most of the monkeys worked out relatively quickly how to get the nuts out of the tubes. But Visalberghi did not take it for granted that the monkeys understood how the tools worked or had any insight into the relationship between what they had done and the outcome. It was not necessarily the case that the monkeys had understood that the stick had displaced the nut and pushed it out of the other end of the tube.

The thing that particularly interested Visalberghi was the errors they made along the way – indicating that they did not have any understanding of how the tools functioned. For instance, some capuchins would insert tiny splinters that clearly couldn't reach the peanuts, and this was when perfectly sized stick were also at their disposal. They would repeatedly try sticks that were far too short or far to thick.

The monkeys eventually succeeded. But, as Visalberghi concluded, the reason they succeeded was because capuchins are quick-moving animals and, and when they try to use sticks in every way possible, they will eventually – through trial and error – hit upon a successful strategy.

In another experiment Visalberghi and Luca Limongelli, a colleague from the National Research Council in Rome, presented capuchins with a transparent tube that had a clearly visible trap hole in the middle with a small transparent cup attached (Visalberghi & Limongelli, 1994). If monkeys have any kind of understanding of gravity they should not push a reward over the trap hole, as the reward would fall into the cup where it would no longer be retrievable. After almost 100 trials only one of the four monkeys learned to push the reward away from the hole rather than over the hole. But when the tube was rotated, so that that the hole was at the top and no longer functioning as a trap, the monkey that had been successful in avoiding the hole carried on using the same strategy. This shows that the monkey lacked any understanding of gravity or the causal relationship between the trap hole and the retrieval of the reward.

Interestingly, Betty, the clever crow who had managed to make a hook in order to retrieve a reward from a vertical tube, when given the same trap hole test only succeeded in retrieving the reward after around 60 trials – indicating that she, like the successful monkey, relied on trial and error learning (Kacelnik *et al.*, 2006). Also, like the capuchin, when the tube was rotated, Betty continued to avoid the 'trap' even though it was now irrelevant. Visalberghi and Tomasello later demonstrated that children as young as three years of age successfully learn to avoid the trap hole after only a few trials (Visalberghi & Tomasello, 1998).

Unlike the capuchins, which only use sticks, chimps use many different kinds of tools for many different purposes in the wild. They use leaves for different purposes – as sponges to soak up drinking water, as umbrellas in heavy rain, or to wipe wounds. They also use sticks to fish for termites and stones to crack open nuts.

Chimps have also been found to modify some tools. Reporting in the journal *Biology Letters* Crickette Sanz of the Max Planck Institute for Evolutionary Anthropology described chimps in the Goualougo Triangle of the Republic of Congo crafting herb stems to scoop insects out of their nests. Prior to fishing for termites, the chimps 'applied a set of deliberate, distinguishable actions to modify herb stems to fashion a brush-tipped probe, which is different from the form of fishing tools used by chimpanzees in East and West Africa' (Sanz *et al.*, 4 March 2009).

According to Richard Byrne:

> the modification of inadequate material until it meets the requirement of a tool shows that chimpanzees, unlike capuchin monkeys, have a mental representation of what a tool needs to be for a certain job (Byrne, 2006: 97).

He adds:

> Certainly, great apes have shown convincingly that their behaviour is not entirely driven by currently observable stimuli. When making tools for food-processing, chimpanzees sometimes fabricate or carefully select the tool in advance and out of sight of the food (Byrne, 2006: 154).

But, despite Byrne's claims, it is still unclear whether chimpanzees have any insight into how the tools they use actually work. They clearly are able to invent more efficient ways of using tools – for instance, a novel, more effective way of fishing for termites. But it seems unlikely that chimps can form mental representations of how the tools work or of what their key design features are. Daniel Povinelli argues in *Folk Physics for Apes: The chimpanzee's theory of how the world works* that apes do not understand the simple, underlying physical principles involved in tool-use. Although apes' understanding of the physical world may appear to be similar to our own, it is in fact profoundly different (Povinelli, 2000). He concludes that 'the more we compare humans and chimpanzees, the more the differences are becoming apparent' (Povinelli, 2004: 31).

Povinelli (2000) points out that there is a fundamental distinction between understanding *that* a tool works and understanding *why* a tool works. For instance, he carried out an experiment on seven chimpanzees, replicating Visalberghi's trap tube test, and found that only one of the chimps performed above chance (Povinelli, 2000). Like the successful capuchin, the successful chimp carried on using the same – now redundant – strategy once the tube had been rotated.

Povinelli and other members of the Cognitive Evolution Group at the University of Louisiana at Lafayette designed a number of further experiments to determine whether chimpanzees are able to reason about things like gravity, weight, mass and physical connection (Povinelli, 2004: 37). Although the apes were quite good at learning to solve problems they were confronted with, they showed little evidence of understanding the underlying, unobservable aspects of the solutions. Instead they appeared to learn rules about the tasks based on directly observable features of success (Vonk & Povinelli, 2006).

One such experiment involved the apes pulling a piece of cloth towards them to obtain an out-of-reach reward lying on top of the cloth. The chimpanzees learnt to retrieve the reward. But follow-up tests established that they merely took into consideration whether the cloth was in contact with the reward, not whether the cloth was underneath the reward (Povinelli, 2000). We would understand that if we are going to use the cloth to pull something towards us the item would need to be on top of the cloth. The chimps hadn't grasped this.

Having reviewed recent experimental results of human and nonhuman tool-use, Derek Penn, affiliate scientist with the Cognitive Evolution Group, and Daniel Povinelli conclude:

> There is not simply an absence of evidence that nonhuman primates possess an intuitive theory about tools, there is also consistent evidence of an absence (Penn & Povinelli, 2007a: 108).

They add:

> While many species (including humans) have a tacit under-standing that some events have the unobservable "power" to cause other events, nonhuman animals causal beliefs appear to be largely content-free: that is, their causal beliefs do not incorporate an abstract representation of the underlying generative mechanisms involved (Penn & Povinelli, 2007a: 110–111).

If they did, wouldn't they keep perfecting the tools they use? And wouldn't this lead to cumulative cultural evolution?

According to Daniel Povinelli, the key difference between apes and humans is that we have the capacity to think about unobservable forces and apes cannot. We can think about 'theoretical things' – that is, 'all the things that are not directly registered to the senses, but are merely posited to exist on the basis of things we can observe', he writes.

Such concepts permeate our common-sense way of thinking: we explain physical events on the basis of things like 'forces' (supernatural or otherwise) that we have never actually witnessed, and account for the behaviour of other humans on the basis of mental states we have never seen (e.g., their beliefs, desires, and emotions) (Povinelli, 2004: 34).

Chimpanzees lack this ability to think about things that are not directly observable, Povinelli argues. As he points out:

If correct, it would mean that chimpanzees do not realise that there is more to others than their movements, their facial expressions, and their habits of behaviour. They would not understand that others are loci of private, internal experience. They would not appreciate that in addition to things that go on in the observable world, there are forever hidden things that go on in the private life of the mind. It would mean that chimpanzees do not reason about what others think, believe, and feel (precisely because they do not form such concepts in the first place) (Povinelli, 2004: 34).

This is a contentious point. Many primatologists have argued that apes do have a Theory of Mind – that is, that they are able to think about thoughts. But the evidence for apes being able to think about what others believe, know and desire is unconvincing, as I will show in the next chapter.

Chapter Four

'Folk Psychology': Are Apes Able to Think About Others' Perceptions, Intentions, Desires and Beliefs?

'I not only use all the brains I have but all I can borrow.'
Woodrow Wilson, (1856–1924)

So what makes human beings uniquely capable of true imitation? Why are we the only species that actively teaches each other? In the groundbreaking book *Ape, Primitive Man and Child*, first published in Russia in 1930, but later suppressed by Stalin, the famous Soviet psychologists Alexander Romanovich Luria and Lev Semyonovich Vygotsky put forward a theoretical framework for explaining what makes us human:

> Our goal has been to outline the three principal lines in the development of behaviour – the evolutionary, the historical and the ontogenetic – and to show that the behaviour of civilised man is the product of all three lines of development and may be understood and explained scientifically only by means of the three distinct paths out of which the history of human behaviour has been formed (Luria & Vygotsky, 1992: xi).

Anthropology, palaeontology, primatology, genetics and other disciplines have given us insights into the possible events in our evolutionary past that created the biological basis for the emergence of our unique abilities. But, as Luria and Vygotsky stress, the evolution of the human genetic make-up is merely the precondition for our humanity.

Our human genetic make-up is very similar to the first *Homo sapiens sapiens* around 150,000–200,000 years ago. But in terms of how we live our lives – our aspirations, values, attitudes, social relationships, knowledge and much more – we are incomparable to our ancestors. Thus, in order to fully understand what shapes us, we need to go beyond the evolutionary line of development. Luria and Vygotsky stressed that we are the product not only of biological evolution but also historical development and individual development, with our unique social relationships.

It is in the area of the third line of development – the ontogenetic or individual line of development – where psychology, and in particular developmental psychology, has made some important strides. At birth, human infants are the product of their biological make-up. As Luria and Vygotsky write:

> In all animals, inherited reactions or innate modes of behaviour form the first stage in the development of behaviour. These are usually called the instinct, and for the most part are associated with the satisfaction of the basic needs of the organism (Luria & Vygotsky, 1992: 1).

But at some point in the child's development, the biological being is transformed into a conscious self-aware being, capable of participating in our collective culture.

The developmental and comparative psychologist Michael Tomasello shows that this is only possible once infants understand other people as intentional beings like themselves. He writes:

> Cultural learning [is] made possible by a single very special form of social cognition, namely, the ability of individual organisms to understand conspecifics as beings *like themselves* who have intentional and mental lives like their own (Tomasello, 1999: 5).

Human beings do not tend to respond blindly to what others do or say, but, constantly – whether consciously or unconsciously – analyse and evaluate others' goals, intentions and motives.

It is this understanding of other beings as beings with intentions that, according to Tomasello, enables children to participate in the world of culture. He writes:

> The outcome is that each child who understands her conspecifics as intentional/mental beings like herself [...] can now participate in the collectivity known as human cognition, and so say (following Isaac Newton) that she sees as far as she does because she 'stands on the shoulders of giants' (Tomasello, 1999: 8).

Because other primates do not have the same capacity to understand intentionality, they do not engage in human-like cultural learning. The human capacity for cultural learning, and our 'collaborative inventiveness', Tomasello argues, 'enable human beings to produce material and symbolic artefacts that build upon one another, and so accumulate modifications through historical time (the ratchet effect), so that human children's cognitive development takes place in the context of something resembling the entire cultural history of their social group' (Tomasello, 1999: 54).

In *The Prehistory of the Mind* Steven Mithen argues that there is an immense evolutionary value to understanding that other people think in the same way as us. The understanding that relations between people involve intentionality could be the key feature that sets our learning apart from non-human primates' acquisition of new skills. But, as Mithen adds 'the corollary of this' is that we find it 'inherently difficult' to think that another animal, and indeed some humans with autism, think 'in a manner that is fundamentally different from our own' (Mithen, 1988: 169).

The idea that our uniqueness rests on our ability to understand our fellows as intentional beings like ourselves suggests there would come a stage in children's early development when their knowledge and understanding of the physical world – in relation to things like space, quantity and causality – would be very similar to those of our nearest primate relatives, but their skills in 'social-cultural cognition' – such as social learning and communication – would already be distinctly human.

To test this hypothesis, researchers at the Max Planck Institute for Evolutionary Anthropology gave a battery of tests to a large number of chimpanzees, orang-utans and human two-year-olds (Herrmann *et al.*, 2007). They found that the young children who had been walking and talking for about a year performed at a similar level to chimpanzees on tasks of physical cognition – such as judging space and quantities and understanding causality – but outstripped both chimpanzees and orang-utans on tasks of social cognition, such as solving a problem by observing someone else doing so first, showing an understanding of the intentions of others, and finding a hidden reward by picking up communication signals.

In one of the social learning, or imitation, tests, the experimenter showed the apes and human children how to open a plastic tube in order to retrieve a reward inside. The children watched the experimenter and imitated the solution. The apes, on the other hand, tried to smash open the tube, or used their teeth to pull its contents out. Lead researcher, Esther Herrmann said:

> Social cognition skills are critical for learning. The children were much better than apes in understanding non-verbal communications, imitating another's solution to a problem, and understanding the intentions of others' (Highfield, 7 September 2007).

The researchers concluded:

> We may thus think of two-year-old children's cognitive development in the physical domain as still basically equivalent to that of the common ancestor of humans and chimpanzees six million years ago (with perhaps a little more sophisticated understanding of causality outside the context of tool use) but their social cognition is already well down the species-specific path' (Herrmann *et al.*, 2008: 1364).

Some scientists argue that even by one year of age, children's performance on imitation tasks goes beyond that of apes: they are able to appreciate that other beings have particular goals. Researchers at the Institute for Psychology at the Hungarian Academy of Sciences showed a group of 14-month-old infants a new way to switch on a light with their forehead (Gergely *et al.*, 2002). In one demonstration the female experimenter's hands were free when she turned on the light with her head. In the other demonstration her hands were occupied: she was holding a blanket around her shoulders. The researchers found that the children only imitated the actions of the experimenter if her action was considered to be intentional. So if the female experimenter's hands were free when she used her head to turn on the light, the infants imitated her actions exactly. But when her hands were occupied – holding the blanket around her shoulders – the children did not tend to imitate her actions exactly, instead opting for the more straightforward alternative of using their hands to switch on the light.

Psychologist György Gergely and colleagues concluded that imitation of goal-directed actions by preverbal children is 'a selective, interpretative process, rather than a simple re-enactment of the means used by a demonstrator, as was previously thought' (Gergely *et al.*, 2002: 755). So rather than simply imitating the actions of a model, pre-verbal children will consider whether there is a reason for carrying out a task in a particular way. If the female experimenter used her head to carry out the task when her hands were free, the infants must have assumed that the use of her head was intentional and therefore that it must serve some purpose; thus they copied the action.

In an experiment by Andrew Meltzoff, co-director of the University of Washington Institute for Learning and Brain Sciences, children were shown an adult trying, but failing, to perform certain actions (Meltzoff, 1995). In one example, the experimenter picked up a stick tool and tried, but failed, to push in the button on a box in order to activate a buzzer inside. In another example, the experimenter tried but failed to pull apart a dumbbell-shaped toy. Meltzoff's aim was to determine whether the children interpreted the model's behaviour in purely physical terms, or whether they were able to look beyond the 'literal body movements' to see the underlying goal of the act. The results indicated that children can indeed infer the adult's goal by watching the failed attempts: they successfully performed the same acts that the adults had apparently intended, but failed, to carry out.

Young children's imitation is therefore guided by an understanding of others' goals and intentions. Their imitation may or may not involve matching the actions performed by another person to achieve a particular goal, depending on whether they perceive the action as intentional or not. Social learning and teaching depends on this ability to understand that other human beings have intentions, and human children gradually begin to develop this ability at the end of their first year.

In reviewing an array of clinical and experimental studies, Peter Hobson, professor of developmental psychopathology and author of *The Cradle of Thought: Exploring the origins of thinking*, captures aspects of human exchanges that happen before language emerges (Hobson, 2002). He shows that even in early infancy children have a capacity to react to the emotions of others. This indicates an innate desire to engage with fellow human beings.

These early emotional engagements were first investigated by the developmental psychologists Jerome Bruner and Michael Scaife in the 1970s. They hit upon the potential significance of what has been coined Joint Attention Episodes (JAE) for children's later development (Scaife & Bruner, 1975). Their groundbreaking research was published in the scientific journal *Nature* in 1975, and since then these episodes have become an important subdiscipline within the field of developmental psychology – now being widely recognised as playing a crucial role in children's development. Bruner and Scaife showed how infants, towards the end of their first year, increasingly follow the gaze of their adult caregivers and begin to monitor the emotional responses of adults in their midst. These JAEs also involve what is referred to as 'proto-declarative pointing': That is, pointing to indicate an object of interest rather than merely pointing to request the object. It is believed that these episodes are based on an awareness of oneself and other people as beings with intentions and goals.

Some hypothesise that JAEs emerge out of an earlier innate desire to engage with other people. For my undergraduate psychology thesis I carried out a small piece of research at Edinburgh University, supervised by the world renowned developmental psychologist Colwyn Trevarthen. Back in the

1970s Trevarthen filmed mothers interacting with their infants on a weekly basis up until they were six months old. After analysing the footage Trevarthen concluded that children are born with a genetic predisposition to engage actively with other people (Trevarthen, 1977). He referred to these early exchanges between an infant and a caregiver – where the infant both takes the initiative and responds to the other person – as 'protoconversations'. Trevarthen and clinical psychologist Kenneth Aitken later described these exchanges thus:

> In the gentle, intimate, affectionate, and rhythmically regulated playful exchanges of protoconversation, 2-month-old infants look at the eyes and mouth of the person addressing them while listening to the voice ... The communicatively active hands of young infants may make expressive movements in rhythmic co-ordination with a person's speech ... and this can occur when the baby has been blind from birth, and thus never seen its hands or anyone else's hands ... Infant and adult can, for a time, sympathise closely and apparently equally with one another's motive states, using similar melodic or prosodic forms of utterance and similar rhythms of gesture (Trevarthen and Aitken, 2001: 6).

Employing Trevarthen's micro-analysis of film and video-records, I also found evidence of an embryonic give-and-take to infants exchanges with their caregivers. When this 'dance', as Trevarthen calls it, between the adult and baby is disrupted by experimental procedures – such as the 'still face' paradigm where the mother is asked to have an impassive and unresponsive 'still' or 'blank' face after having communicated cheerfully – the infant expresses withdrawal and distress (Tronick, 2005).

Later in the child's first year these protoconversations are turned into Joint Attention Episodes, where the interactions between the infant and caregiver begin to refer to objects or events. As Hobson writes, the infant 'registers that the other person is connected not just with herself, but with objects and events in the world. She is interested in what the other person does with things and feels towards things' (Hobson, 2002: 62–63). He adds a note of caution: we should hold back from supposing that infants at this early stage have conscious thoughts and understandings of other people as beings they can share experiences with. But with development, these innate desires are transformed into something qualitatively different. By the middle of the second year of life infants' early emotional engagements are transformed into more conscious exchanges of feelings, desires, views and beliefs.

JAEs are therefore only the beginning of a revolution in children's development, Hobson argues. He writes:

> I say this is the *beginning* of a revolution, because at the beginning the infant does not know in an intellectual way that the world has a meaning for others. The discovery is a discovery in action and feeling, rather than a discovery in thought (Hobson, 2002: 73).

Significantly, the end of the first year is also the time children first start to learn through imitation. Indeed, during the next couple of years of their lives young children could be described as 'imitation machines': they constantly copy people around them, and their natural response to a challenge is to look at what others in their midst are doing.

An experiment carried out in the United States in the 1930s by the psychologist Winthrop Kellogg and his wife Luella gives us an insight into the power of imitation in young children's early development. The Kelloggs decided to rear an infant female chimpanzee, Gua, with their own infant son, Donald, under conditions as identical as possible (Kellogg and Kellogg, 1933). Their aim was to investigate how 'human' a chimpanzee would become if reared as a human. When the experiment started Gua was 7 months of age and Donald 10 months of age. They were both tested on a daily basis on a host of different measures such as memory, vocalisation, locomotion, manual dexterity, problem solving, language comprehension, attention span, and much more.

In terms of motor skills, such as climbing and jumping, Gua developed at a much faster rate than Donald. She also learned to respond to a number of words and phrases such as 'shake hands' and 'show me your nose' earlier than Donald did. Gua never learnt to speak but was able to make some of her wishes known through grunts and squeals. Although

Gua progressed faster than Donald in the first months of the study, by the middle of the second year of life the chimp was falling behind. The study came to an abrupt halt after just 9 months.

Psychologists Ludy Benjamin and Darryl Bruce speculate that the reason for the termination of the research project was the effect it was having on the researchers' own son. Not only was Donald's language seriously retarded but he had started to grunt like an ape. They write:

> While Gua did not imitate Donald's sounds, the opposite was not true. When Donald was 14 months of age, the Kelloggs first observed him imitating the food bark that Gua would use in the presence of food. Initially he would mimic Gua's calls while she was engaged in such vocalisations, but later he would initiate the sounds wholly on his own (Benjamin & Bruce 1982: 471).

The husband and wife team therefore not only found that by bringing up an ape like a human it will not become human, but much to their unease they saw first-hand the imitative tendency of a human child – resulting in their son adopting many rather disturbing ape-like behaviours.

Human children not only are able to learn through collaboration and imitation, but by the time they are around four years of age they are drawing much more upon what Lev Vygotsky coined 'cultural tools', such as language, to allow them to plan and reflect upon their own actions in a more conscious manner (Vygotsky, 1978). Building upon Vygotsky's insights, Tomasello argues that human cognition does not emerge fully formed:

> To the contrary, the human understanding of others as intentional beings makes its initial appearance at around nine months of age, but its real power becomes apparent only gradually as children actively employ the cultural tools that this understanding enables them to master, most importantly language (Tomasello, 1999: 56).

It is out of the earlier Joint Attention Episodes that language – and with it thought – emerges. But also, these early exchanges are believed to be the basis for the development of a full-blown Theory of Mind, that is the ability to recognise that one's own perspectives and beliefs can be different from someone else's and different from one's own previous beliefs.

The term Theory of Mind was coined by the psychologist David Premack and primatologist Guy Woodruff in 1978 in their seminal paper *Does the Chimpanzee Have a Theory of Mind?* (Premack & Woodruff, 1978). Premack and Woodruff wanted to find out whether chimpanzees had an understanding of more than just surface-level behaviour – that is, the behaviour that they can actually see. Or do chimps understand what goes on beneath the surface and have insights into the goals, perceptions, knowledge and the beliefs that may guide the actions of those they engage with? Premack later concluded that the evidence for chimps having a Theory of Mind is 'painfully thin' (Premack, 1988: 176).

I will return to the rather murky evidence for and against apes having a Theory of Mind, but in relation to children, the picture has become a lot clearer since Premack and Woodruff's paper was first published. We have learnt a lot in recent years about infants' and toddlers' ability to think about unobservable forces such as goals, intentions, perceptions, knowledge and beliefs.

It has been found that children don't tend to be able to think about other people's knowledge and beliefs until they are around four years old. As part of the research for my PhD on child development, I carried out a Theory of Mind test on children between three and four in a primary school in Manchester. I presented the children, one of whom I shall call Mark, with a tube of Smarties. When I asked Mark what he thought was inside the tube his face lit up. 'Smarties!' he exclaimed. I handed him the tube and asked him to look inside. His face quickly fell when he realised that what was inside was not Smarties after all, but crayons. I then told Mark that after he had gone back to the classroom one of his classmates, Mary, would come into the room to play the same game with me. 'I will show Mary this tube and ask her what she thinks is inside. What do you think she'll say?' Mark, like most children under four, said, 'Crayons.' He knew, after having looked inside, that the tube of Smarties actually contained crayons, so of course Mary would say it contained crayons too.

When I asked him what he thought was inside the tube before he opened it he again said, 'Crayons.' Mark could not contemplate that knowledge and beliefs can be different from reality. He had found out that the tube contained crayons and was incapable of differentiating his current knowledge and belief from what another child may believe or even from what he believed before he opened the tube of Smarties. He was not yet capable of thinking about thoughts. Once children are able to think about thoughts, their thinking is lifted to a different level.

Recent research indicates that a Theory of Mind is not an all-or-nothing phenomenon. Children may not understand that other people can have different knowledge and beliefs from themselves until they are around four years old, but they do grasp – at a much younger age – that other people may have different desires from themselves.

In his 1989 book *Children and Emotion: The development of psychological understanding* Paul Harris, professor of education at Harvard Graduate School, describes stories about imaginary animal characters told to pre-school children in order to find out whether they were able to think and reason about desires. One of the stories was about a puppet called Ellie the Elephant who was a fussy drinker, only liking milk. One day when Ellie was out for a walk she got very thirsty. She was looking forward to returning from her walk so she could drink her favourite drink. But while she was out for her walk a mischievous puppet, Naughty Monkey, had poured the milk out of the carton and filled it up with coke. Ellie, of course, was unaware of what Naughty Monkey had done.

After hearing the story, the children were asked how they thought Ellie felt when she returned home to see her carton, before taking a swig out of it. Many four years olds answered correctly that Ellie would be 'excited' or 'pleased' when seeing the carton she was about to drink from, because they correctly understood that Ellie both desired a drink of milk and wrongly believed that the carton contained milk. They also said that she would be sad when she tasted the drink because she only liked milk.

The three year olds on the other hand tended to answer that Ellie would be angry or disappointment when seeing her carton as they did not understand that Ellie – who had not witnessed Naughty Monkey filling the carton with coke – had the mistaken belief that the carton contained milk. They knew what was in the carton and automatically assumed that Ellie had the same knowledge. This shows that the three year olds did have the capacity to understand that others may have different *desires* from themselves, and that certain events can make others sad, even if those same events would not make them sad, but they found it difficult to reason about others' knowledge and beliefs.

In fact, an interesting experiment carried out by the developmental psychologists Betty Rapocholi and Alison Gopnik showed that children as young as 18 months of age can show an understanding of others' desires (Rapocholi & Gopnik, 1997). Two bowls of food were presented to 14 and 18-month-old children individually. One bowl contained raw broccoli and the other contained crackers. When encouraged to help themselves the majority of children took crackers, indicating that they preferred the crackers to the raw broccoli. The experimenter would then help herself from both bowls, feigning disgust when tasting the crackers and delight when tasting the raw broccoli. Afterwards she would put her hand out and ask 'can you give me some more?'. The 18-month-olds took their cues from her earlier reaction and gave her what she had indicated that she preferred, even though they themselves clearly preferred the crackers. The 14-month-olds 'responded egocentrically' and offered her 'whichever food they themselves preferred' (Rapocholi & Gopnik, 1997: 12).

As the researchers concluded:

> These data constitute the first empirical evidence that 18-month-olds are able to engage in some form of desire reasoning. Children not only inferred that another person held a desire, but also recognised how desires are related to emotions (Rapocholi & Gopnik, 1997: 12).

Strong claims have been put forward about apes' social intelligence. In 2007 Zoologist Charlotte Uhlenbroek told *BBC News*:

If I were an alien from Mars and looked at human society and a society of apes then in terms of the emotional life I would see no distinct difference, although we live very different lives because of language and technology (*BBC News*, 2007).

Similarly, science writer Mark Henderson writes: 'The similarities between chimpanzees and humans have been revealed further by research suggesting that our closest cousins are capable of empathy' (Henderson, 9 September 2008). He was commenting on a British Association Science Festival presentation by Orlaith Fraser of Liverpool John Moores University, who had spent 18 months observing 22 adult chimps at Chester Zoo. Fraser claimed that the apes' tendency to 'console' other apes after they had been involved in a fight could indicate some level of empathy, but did concede: 'We can't actually say what's going on in a chimpanzee's mind; we can only deduce from their behaviour what's going on.'

Frans de Waal, of Emory University in Atlanta, USA, said: 'The present study is significant in that it suggests that the function of this behaviour in chimpanzees is similar to humans, in that it comforts the other.' In his 2005 book *Our Inner Ape* de Waal recounts an anecdotal observation at George State University Language Research Center in Atlanta involving the language-trained bonobo Kanzi, with a 'fabulous understanding of spoken English', and his non-comprehending sister, Tamuli. De Waal writes:

> Realising that some of his fellow apes do not have the same training, Kanzi occasionally adopts the role of teacher. He once sat next to Tamuli, a younger sister who had minimal exposure to human speech, while a researcher tried to get Tamuli to respond to simple verbal requests; the untrained bonobo didn't respond. As the researcher addressed Tamuli, it was Kanzi who began to act out the meanings (de Waal, 2005:7).

In claiming that Kanzi showed an understanding of his sister's lack of knowledge, de Waal implies that the bonobo has a full-blown a Theory of Mind. De Waal writes:

> Kanzi understands perfectly well whether commands are intended for him or for others. He was not carrying out a

command intended for Tamuli, but he actually tried to make her understand. Kanzi's sensitivity to his sister's lack of knowledge, and his kindness in teaching her, suggests a level of empathy found, as far as we know, only in humans and apes (de Waal, 2005:7).

In *Through a Window: Thirty years with the chimpanzees of Gombe* Jane Goodall provides further anecdotal evidence of apes having a Theory of Mind. She describes how the 'adolescent' Figan, one of the chimpanzees she studied, 'had learned to stay behind in camp after senior males had left, so that we could give him a few bananas for himself'. She writes:

> On the first occasion he had, upon seeing the fruits, uttered loud, delighted food calls: whereupon a couple of the older males had charged back, chased after Figan, and taken his bananas. [On] the next occasion, Figan had actually suppressed his calls. We could hear little sounds in his throat, but so quiet that none of the others could have heard them (Goodall 1990: 12).

This implies that Figan was deliberately trying to deceive his fellows. Goodall also observed a chimp who had spotted fruit in a tree actively refraining from approaching it or drawing attention to it by looking at it, until the other chimps had left the area (Goodall, 1971). Other primatologists have observed apes in the wild giving alarm calls when no danger is present, with the effect of distracting another animal from food or a mate.

If apes really do attempt to deceive their fellows, this does point towards what some have described as a Machiavellian intelligence. But, as I have argued in earlier chapters, anecdotal evidence can be highly deceptive. Even if there was consistent evidence that apes deceive their fellows, the question still remains whether they are aware of what they are doing. Deception itself does not necessarily imply intentionality. To be able to deceive intentionally, an animal would need to be able to think about the intentions, knowledge and beliefs of those they are deceiving. In other words, they would need to have a Theory of Mind.

There are many examples of deception in the wild that clearly does not involve a Theory of Mind. Take the Eyed

Hawk-moth: when threatened or startled, it flaps open its wings to reveal large eyespots. But, as evolutionary psychologist Richard Byrne points out:

> Moths react to looming cardboard squares and to looming animals that could eat them, alike; they expose their huge 'eyes' to small animals, that might plausible be frightened by hawks, and to big ones, including real hawks. So we have real reason to doubt that they understand about mental states of predators (Byrne, 2006: 123).

Byrne also explored examples of pets seemingly deceiving their owners, showing again, that there is not necessarily any intentionality involved in their deception. Some pet owners have reported that their cats sometimes go to the door and meow, as if wishing to go outside, but as soon as the owner gets out of their warm cosy chair to let the cat out, the cat 'steals' their seat. This cannot be explained on the basis of an evolutionary adapted trait – in the way the 'eyes' on the Hawk-moth can – but can be explained on the basis of contingent learning or conditioning.

Byrne writes:

> Suppose only that the cat, in the past, genuinely wanted to go outside, but not as much as it wanted to sleep by the fire. Thwarted of its priority goal, it switched to the second alternative, and mewed at the door. However, just then, the chair became vacant (which we, but not the cat, realise was because the owner believed the cat needed urgently to go outside, and got up to help), and the cat was able to revert to its major aim. This highly plausible history would serve to condition the cat's future use of the tactic (Byrne, 2006: 130–131).

He concludes:

> In general, interactions with loving humans in a built environment give ample opportunities for trial and error learning to proceed from lucky coincidences, explaining why domestic carnivores seem more deceptive than their wild relatives (Byrne, 2006: 131).

So even if apes are found to deceive, that does not necessarily imply that they know that they are deceiving. The apes may just be very good at picking up useful routines that bring them food, sex or safety, without necessarily having any understanding or insight into what they are doing. Having reviewed a wealth of data, Byrne concludes that unlike other primates great apes do show evidence of a Theory of Mind. He points out that they have passed artificial laboratory tasks, and use the capability in natural circumstances – for instance to deceive other apes. Curiously, deception is more common among some monkeys than apes in the wild. But, according to Byrne, monkeys do not have a Theory of Mind. Instead deception among monkeys can be explained by rapid trial-and-error learning, 'the sophistication of ape deception marks it out,' he argues (Byrne, 2006: 144).

But comparative cognitive psychologist, Daniel Povinelli, who runs the Cognitive Evolution Group at the University of Louisiana at Lafayette, is now unequivocal in arguing that no test to date has reliably demonstrated that chimpanzees – or any other nonhuman primate for that matter – have an understanding of the mental life of others. He writes: 'At present there is no direct evidence that chimpanzees conceive of mental states, and considerable indirect evidence that they do not' (Povinelli, 2004: 35).

To investigate chimps' so-called understanding of 'folk psychology', Povinelli tested whether chimps understood that their begging gestures would only be effective if the person they were begging from could actually see them. He designed experiments examining how chimpanzees would respond to caretakers who either obviously could and could not see them. For example, one caretaker had a blindfold covering her mouth and the other had a blindfold covering her eyes.

He found that the chimpanzees did not differentiate between the caretaker who could clearly see them (the one with the blindfold over her mouth) and the caretaker who could not see them (the one with the blindfold over her eyes) when making begging gestures. Similar tests with human children found that even two-year-olds gestured to the person with the blindfold over their mouth rather than the one with the blindfold over their eyes – indicating an awareness that only the person with the blindfold over their mouth could see them (Povinelli, 2001).

In another experiment Povinelli and cognitive psychologist Jennifer Vonk again found that the chimps showed no preference when making begging gestures to caretakers when one wore see-through visors and the other opaque visors (Povinelli & Vonk, 2003; Penn & Povinelli, 2007b). In a training session the participants were given first-hand experience of wearing the visors which were clearly differentiated by having different colours and shapes. All the human-reared chimpanzees failed the tests. But human infants as young as 18-month of age passed a similar test with trick blindfolds (Meltzoff, 2004).

Penn and Povinelli write:

> These results would seem to provide positive confirmatory evidence that even young human infants possess some sort of Theory of Mind whereas even highly enculturated adult chimpanzees do not (Penn & Povinelli, 2007b: 740).

Povinelli did not always believe that apes lacked a Theory of Mind. In an earlier experiment, he and co-workers tested the mental abilities of monkeys and apes, and concluded, like Byrne, that apes but not monkeys have a Theory of Mind. Four chimpanzees and four rhesus monkeys were presented with conflictual advice – by means of pointing – from two humans, one who had clearly seen where food had been hidden and one who had not (Povinelli *et al.*,1990). This was to test whether the primates would follow the advice of the 'knower' or the 'guesser', after being presented with 10 trials a day over several weeks. Three of the chimpanzees fairly consistently selected the advice of the 'knower', while none of the rhesus monkeys discriminated between the 'knower' and the 'guesser'.

But comparative psychologist Michael Tomasello questioned whether these findings indicated that apes have a Theory of Mind, or even its precursor, an understanding of intentionality. He pointed out that the problem with many experiments – such as this early experiment by Povinelli and colleagues – was that the apes only learned to differentiate between a 'knower' and a 'guesser' after many trials. Tomasello argued:

[T]he chimpanzees in these studies did not seem to bring a knowledge of others' intentionality or mentality to the experiment, but rather learned how to behave to get what they wanted as the experiment unfolded (Tomasello, 1999: 20).

When Michael Tomasello and Josep Call, at the Max Planck Institute for Evolutionary Anthropology, gave a similar task to seven chimpanzees and orang-utans – where they ruled out any possibility of a learning effect – none of the apes succeeded in the task, thereby showing no understanding of the knowledge of others (Tomasello & Call, 1999). Whereas when Povinelli gave the same test to four-year-old human children, they performed at 'a near-perfect levels from the first trial forward' (Povinelli, 1996: 290).

In recent years Povinelli and his team in the Cognitive Evolution Group at the University of Louisiana have become increasingly sceptical about the ability of apes to reason about what goes on inside the head of their fellows. At the same time Tomasello and his colleagues at the Max Planck Institute for Evolutionary Anthropology have been swayed in the other direction – arguing that apes, like humans, do seem to have something that other primates lack.

The Cognitive Evolution Group argues that apes may pass certain Theory of Mind tests, not because they have the ability to take into account the perspectives and beliefs of others, but instead because they are adept at learning from *observable* behaviour. The team has put forward persuasive arguments against apes' ability to reason about *unobservable* forces, such as desires, intentions, knowledge and beliefs. 'Mind-reading' is unique to human beings, they argue (Penn & Povinelli, 2007b: 733).

Penn and Povinelli have critically examined a key experiment – one that has been cited by many as 'breakthrough' evidence that chimpanzees understand some psychological states in others – and concluded that the most likely explanation was that the chimps responded to observable behaviour. The experiment was designed by Michael Tomasello and Josep Call, with Brian Hare, assistant professor in the Department of Biological Anthropology and Anatomy at Duke University, and Bryan Agnetta, from the Yerkes Regional Primate Research

Center at Emory University (Hare *et al.*, 2001; Tomasello *et al.*, 2003).

Two chimpanzees – one dominant and one subordinate – were kept in separate rooms on opposite sides of a middle chamber in which small food items were hidden in two cloth bags. Each of the side rooms had guillotine doors leading to the middle chamber. The chimpanzees were not able to enter the chamber until the guillotine doors were completely raised. On each trial the door of the subordinate was partially raised, allowing her to peek while a human hid the food items in the middle chamber. On some trials the dominant's door was closed and on others it was partially raised. Therefore, on some occasions, but not all, the dominant could also peek while the food was placed in the bags. The subordinate was able to see whether or not the dominant's door was partially open and was always given a head start when the chimps were released into the chamber.

Hare and colleagues predicted that 'if the subordinates were sensitive to what others have or have not seen, they should more often approach and retrieve the food when the dominant was uninformed about its location' (Hare *et al.*, 2001: 141). Indeed, the subordinate chimps did go for the food that only they could see much more often than for the food that both they and the dominant could see. Hare and colleagues postulated that 'chimpanzees do indeed know what conspecifics can and cannot see, and that they use this knowledge in food competition situations' (Hare *et al.*, 2001: 140).

When their experiment was first published Hare and colleagues added the rider that they 'prefer to remain cautious' with regards to conclusions drawn from their study because interpretation is difficult when tasks are non-verbal. However several years later Call and Tomasello argued that there is solid evidence from several different experimental paradigms that chimpanzees understand the goals and intentions of others, as well as the perception and knowledge of others (Call & Tomasello, 2008a: 187). They wrote:

> It is time for humans to quit thinking that their nearest primate relatives only read and react to overt behaviour. Obviously,

chimpanzees' social understanding begins with the observation of others' behaviour, as it does for humans, but it does not end there. Even if chimpanzees do not understand false beliefs, they clearly do not just perceive the surface behaviour of others and learn mindless behavioural rules as a result (Call & Tomasello, 2008a: 187).

After examining the findings of Hare and colleagues, however, Penn and Povinelli argue that although it may be 'intuitively appealing' to conclude from these findings that the subordinate chimpanzees could reason about what the dominant chimpanzees did and did not know, such a conclusion would in fact be causally superfluous. Instead the subordinates' behaviour could be explained on the basis of them simply using observable information from past behavioural patterns: The chimpanzees may have learnt from past events not to go after food if a dominant has been 'oriented towards it' (Penn & Povinelli, 2007b: 738). There is no evidence that they are able to think about what is going on inside the heads of the dominant chimpanzees. Penn and Povinelli conclude:

> The available evidence suggests that chimpanzees and all other non-human animals only form representations and reason about *observable* features, relations and states of affairs from their own cognitive perspective. We know of no evidence that non-human animals are capable of representing or reasoning about *unobservable* features, relations, causes or states of affairs or of constructing information from the cognitive perspective of another agent (Penn & Povinelli, 2007b: 739).

Although there is no substantive evidence of apes having a Theory of Mind, they may possess one of its precursors – a rudimentary self-awareness. This is backed up by the fact that, apart from human beings, great apes are the only species able to recognise themselves in the mirror.

Writing a story about how Rwanda's Virunga mountain gorillas had lived through decades of war, *Daily Mail* science editor Michael Hanlon ended up following a breakaway group of two not-quite-mature females and a young male who 'looked for all the world like a group of teenage friends going for a walk' (Hanlon, 2007: 19). Hanlon followed them to a small gorge, where he found one of the females staring 'very intently at her reflections' in a small pond. He writes:

> I could swear she ran her digits through her hair, looking at her face in the water-mirror as she did so. Then one of the others, also staring at the reflections, jabbed a hand into the water, which of course broke up into ripples. At that point the three animals fell about, laughing at their now-wobbly reflections (Hanlon, 2007: 19)

Recognising that some scientists might turn their noses up at this anecdotal story, with its anthropomorphic descriptions, Hanlon writes:

> A proper scientist, as opposed to a journalist or tourist, would no doubt describe their change in posture and body attitude using very different terms than 'falling about'. 'Who knows what is going through their minds?', scientists would say, so best not go there. I'm sorry but this will not do. Sometimes, if it looks like a duck, walks like a duck and quacks like a duck it is easier just to assume you are in fact dealing with a duck, rather than some sort of complex analogy. These gorillas were falling about laughing at what passes for entertainment in the Virunga forests. And if a sense of humour is not a sign of intelligence and self-awareness, it is hard to see what is (Hanlon, 2007: 19–20).

In 1970, the professor of psychology, Gordon Gallup, devised what has become known as the 'mirror self-recognition test' (Gallup, 1970). The test sets out to determine whether an animal or human being can recognise that its own reflection in a mirror is indeed an image of itself, rather than another being. Gallup exposed a group of chimpanzees to mirrors, finding that at first they responded to their reflection in the mirror as if it was another animal. But after a few days the chimps behaved as though they realised that their reflection in the mirror was indeed a reflection of themselves.

To test whether this really was the case, Gallup surreptitiously marked the chimps with two odourless non-irritant dye spots on parts of their bodies they could not see other than in a mirror. One spot was marked on their brow above one eye and the other on the top half of the opposite ear.

Observations of the chimps behaviour in the absence of the mirror confirmed that they had no knowledge of the marks, as they rarely touched the spots. But, as Gallup writes:

When the mirror was reinstated, however, the effect was dramatic: the chimpanzees looked at their reflection and guided their fingers to the marks on their faces that could only be seen in the mirror. In addition to touching the marks repeatedly and looking at their fingers, some even smelled their fingers (Gallup *et al.*, 2002: 335).

A number of studies have since been taken as evidence that chimpanzees and orang-utans, but not gorillas, can recognise themselves in the mirror (Suarez and Gallup, 1981). The only gorilla that has been claimed to pass the mirror self-recognition test is Koko, a gorilla brought up by human beings from an early age (Patterson & Cohn, 1994).

In developmental literature, the moment when human infants first recognise themselves in the mirror (between 15 and 21 months of age) is seen as an important milestone in the emergence of the notion of 'self'. How important is it, then, that apes may be able to make the same sort of mirror recognition?

Psychologist Cecilia Heyes has not only questioned whether apes have any concept of self, but even whether they are capable of self-recognition. She carried out a review of the mirror–recognition research initiated by Gallup and concluded that no animal has been shown to be capable of self-recognition in mirror tests. She suggested that in Gallup's initial test, the chimpanzees may have begun touching their marks when the mirror was brought back, not because they recognised themselves, but simply because the anaesthetic used to sedate them while they were marked began to wear off at about the same time (Heyes, 1994). In the mirror-present condition the apes were generally more active, which backs up her claim.

The development of human children's self-awareness is a complex process with different elements emerging at different times. Mirror recognition is only the precursor to a continually developing capacity for self-awareness and self-evaluation. The ability of apes to recognise themselves in the mirror does not necessarily imply a human-like self-awareness or the existence of mental experiences. They may be able to represent their own bodies visually, but they never move beyond the stage reached by human children in their second year of life.

Indeed, taking inspiration from one of the fathers of psychology, William James, Heyes argues:

> Humans with a 'self concept' are commonly assumed, not only to know where their body ends and the rest of the world begins (the 'material' self), but also to have certain beliefs about their fate and moral standing (the 'spiritual self'), and about the way in which they are regarded by others (the 'social' self). While it may well be true that these three types of knowledge or beliefs co-exist in humans, there is no necessary logical link between them (Heyes, 1994: 915).

Chapter Five
Language and Communication

'Thought is the blossom; language the bud; action the fruit behind it.'
Ralph Waldo Emerson, (1803–1882).

Talking to the *New York Times*, the world renowned primatologist, Sue Savage-Rumbaugh, claimed:

> [Apes in the wild] do make all kinds of ape noises. And I believe they use them to communicate with one another. Now, the apes may not always elect to talk about the same things we do. They might not have a translation for every word in our vocabulary to theirs. But from what I've seen, I believe they are communicating very complex things (Dreifus, 1998).

There is no doubt that apes and other animals are able to communicate with each other in the wild – whether through courtship rituals, dominance and territorial displays, or food and alarm calls. For instance, dogs bare their teeth and growl to signal to other animals to leave their territory. Cats try to make themselves look bigger and more menacing by puffing out the hair on their tails to signal to other animals not to oppose them. Subordinate chimpanzees use grunts directed to dominant chimpanzees to signal appeasement or submission. However, the evidence for any animal being able to communicate 'very complex things' is non-existent.

Despite animals being incapable of communicating anything remotely complex, the means by which some species communicate with each other can appear extremely elaborate. Take the honey bee. Through its 'waggle-dance' it is able to communicate to its hive-mates in which direction and how far they must fly to find water, pollen or nectar. The bee indicates the direction of the food source through the angle from the sun, and the distance to the food source through the duration of the waggle.

Neither the honey bees waggle-dance nor primates cries, whoops and gestures are comparable with human language. Robbins Burling, professor of anthropology and linguistics at the University of Michigan, writes in *The Talking Ape: How language evolved*:

> Like most other mammals, primates communicate with their voices as well as by movements and gestures. With their cries, whoops and chatter they coordinate their activities, call for help, show their anger, make threats, and even warn one another of danger. Since most human languages are also produced with the voice, and since language is also used to coordinate activites, call for help, and show emotions, hardly anyone can resist searching among primates calls for the forerunners of human language (Burling, 2005: 16).

But although it may seem reasonable to ask how natural selection might have transformed these more primitive forms of communication into the kind of language that humans speak, such an investigation would be fruitless, Burling argues. He writes:

> Language is organised in such utterly different ways from primate or mammalian calls and it conveys such utterly different kinds of meanings, that I find it impossible to imagine a realistic sequence by which natural or sexual selection could have converted a call system into a language. Human beings, moreover still have a fine set of primate calls that remains quite separate from language. Primate calls have much less in common with human language than with howls, screams, sighs, sobs, and laughter (Burling, 2005: 16).

Similarly, language expert Joel Wallman argues: 'The received wisdom in primate studies, which has been endorsed at various points in [my] work, is that the calls of prosimians, monkeys and apes are, for the most part or entirely, affective in signification' (Wallman, 1992: 133). That is, most communications are driven by primitive emotions. There are exceptions, Wallman concedes, such as the honey bee's waggle-dance and the 'food call' of the chimpanzee, but the best evidence for animals' ability to communicate information to their fellows in the wild comes from field studies of monkeys' communications.

Groundbreaking research on vervet monkeys in the wild by Robert Seyfarth and Dorothy Cheney in the 1980s showed that the monkeys' vocalisations and communications clearly go beyond merely expressing instinctive reactions similar to anger or fear. Their vocalisations could instead be described as 'referential' in that they refer to particular objects or events.

Living on the edge of the savannah, vervet monkeys have many predators. Their chance of survival would therefore be greatly increased if they were able to respond appropriately to different vocal warnings. Indeed, it was found that the vervets have specific alarm calls for specific predators: the alarm call for an eagle is different from that for a leopard, which in turn is different from that for a python (Seyfarth *et al.*, 1980). Seyfarth and Cheney made recordings of the monkeys' vocalisations and later broadcast those recordings from a hidden tape recorder in the wild. They found that each alarm call elicited a different reaction from the monkeys, even when no predator was present. On hearing the alarm call for an eagle the monkeys would look up and flee into the bushes for cover. While on hearing the alarm-call for a leopard they would seek safety in a tree. And on hearing the alarm-call for a python would scan the ground and mob together.

From the outset of their study, Seyfarth and Cheney stressed that it could not be established from these initial findings whether the callers vocalised with the explicit intent of referring to the proximity of a predator. They were careful to point out that there was no evidence that the monkeys had 'thoughts' that they intentionally conveyed to others – such as 'Oh no! I see a dangerous leopard. I had better warn the others quickly and make sure that they know it is a predator that may get us unless we seek safety in a tree'.

Later experiments have attempted to refine analyses in order to establish whether there is an intention to communicate, or any voluntary control of vocalisations. It has been found that all vervets have the same basic vocal repertoire and make all the alarm calls from an early age – and infants are found to use alarm calls indiscriminately at first, such as making an eagle alarm call in response to anything flying, even a falling leaf. It is therefore believed that the monkeys are genetically predisposed to respond to specific stimuli with specific alarm calls.

When it comes to vervet monkeys, the best way of understanding their communications is as instinctual vocalisations rather than language that is acquired, though they might be refined over time through some form of learning. Indeed, Wallman argues that: 'The bulk of a monkey's or ape's repertoire of calls are inborn; their development seems not to require exposure to conspecifics' (Wallman, 1992: 142). Researchers have found that even when separated from their fellows, many monkeys and apes will still develop their species specific calls (Call & Tomasello, 2008b; Tomasello, 2008). In *Origins of Human Communications*, Michael Tomasello argues that 'the reason for this lack of flexibility in vocal production is that nonhuman primate vocalisations are mostly tightly tied to emotions' (Tomasello, 2008: 17). He writes:

> Evolutionarily, this is because vocal calls are often associated with especially urgent functions such as escaping predators, surviving in fights, keeping contact with the group, and so forth. In such cases urgent action is needed, and there is little time for thoughtful deliberation. In all cases, each particular call has been selected evolutionarily because it benefits the caller in some way (Tomasello, 2008: 17).

The caller's vocalisations are not 'intended' for other animals. Tomasello demonstrates that the vervets' alarm calls benefits the caller – by for instance distracting the predator – and that the other vervets are merely informed by 'eavesdropping'. This was demonstrated by Cheney and Seyfarth in experiments where vervet mothers would see 'predators' approaching their offspring. The mothers would not give the alarm calls unless they themselves were at risk (Cheney & Seyfarth, 1990). This indicates that vervets do not 'understand' a threat, but simply respond instinctively to certain stimuli.

All this helps explain why early ape language projects singularly failed to teach apes to talk. Almost a century ago, William Furness finally succeeded in teaching a young orangutan to utter the words 'papa' and 'cup' after hour upon hour of training, placing his fingers on the ape's lips and moulding the lip movements. A few decades later Keith and Catherine Hayes tried to teach Viki, their home-raised chimpanzee, to speak. After more than six years of laborious training they succeeded in teaching Viki to say just four words – 'mama,' 'papa,' 'cup' and 'up.'

The apes' failure to speak is partly due to apes' vocal tracts not being capable of producing the range of sounds of a human language. However these apes did show that they could 'understand' – or, as Winthrop Kellogg stated, 'react characteristically to' – spoken language (Kellogg, 1968: 425). In the first four months of Winthrop and Luella Kellogg's study – where they compared the abilities of their home-raised chimpanzee, Gua, with the abilities of their infant son, Donald – they found that the chimpanzee was ahead of their son in the number of spoken phrases to which she was able to respond appropriately. These phrases varied from very simple commands, such as 'come here', to slightly more complex commands, such as 'close the door,' or 'go to mama.' The ape's head start may have been due to apes motor-skills developing quicker than human infants'. Donald may have 'understood' the commands, but just wasn't able to carry out the commands. In the last five months of the study Donald rapidly surpassed Gua in language comprehension tasks.

In the past couple of decades, ape language studies have abandoned attempts to teach apes to speak and have focused instead on gestural or invented visual languages. The accomplishments of the apes using American Sign Language (ASL) and other visual language systems have been a lot more impressive than were the early language studies.

In the 1960s the husband and wife team Allen and Beatrix Gardner, a psychologist and an ethologist, began a project to teach an infant female chimpanzee, Washoe, to communicate using sign language. Washoe was born in the wild and acquired by the Gardners when she was around one year old. She was housed in a trailer in the their backyard, but otherwise was brought up like a human child. She was taught American Sign Language through a moulding technique, where her hands were physically guided into the correct position, as she did not seem to acquire signs through imitation. After four years of training she was able to sign 132 words.

'Washoe learned a natural human language and her early utterances were highly similar to, perhaps indistinguishable from the early utterances of human children', the Gardners claimed (Gardner and Gardner, 1978: 73). However, more remarkably, Loulis, Washoe's adopted son, who was placed with her when he was 10 months old, learned 22 signs without any instruction from human beings. By watching Washoe sign, he seems to have learnt to make requests, such as 'tickle', 'drink' and 'hug'.

A few years later, another study began at the Yerkes Primate Laboratory in Atlanta. Rather than use sign-language, Duane Rumbaugh, a comparative psychologist, taught a juvenile chimpanzee Lana to use an artificial visual language, named Yerkish, using computer keys to represent words. Lana, unlike, Washoe, was caged during the language lessons. By composing a sequence of 'lexigrams' on her keyboard that were deemed grammatically acceptable Lana could get her computer to dispense food and drink. In order to get a drink she would need to press the lexigrams in the order 'Please machine give drink'. She could also communicate with her trainers, for instance to request them to tickle or groom her.

Rumbaugh and his wife, the primatologist Sue Savage-Rumbaugh, have since dedicated their lives to teaching great apes to use arbitrary visual symbols as a means of communication. Savage-Rumbaugh was the first scientist to conduct language research with bonobos, the most famous of which is Kanzi. The first bonobo she began teaching was a wild-caught female bonobo named Matata. Although Matata singularly failed to adopt Yerkish, the trainers found that her son, Kanzi, who had been at her side throughout her first two years of language instruction, had acquired an ability to use the lexigram system.

The first language study with an orang-utan was carried out by the anthropologist Lyn Miles on an infant male, named Chantek (meaning 'beautiful' in Malaysian), who, like Washoe, was raised as a human child in a trailer on the University of Tennessee Chattanooga campus. By eight years of age Chantek had learned approximately 150 signs.

But the ape that is widely seen as *the* leading light of the ape language world is the gorilla named Koko. The Californian Gorilla Foundation, established in 1976, boasts that it has carried out 'groundbreaking work' with western lowland gorillas, including Koko, who were taught to 'become fluent in American Sign Language' (The Gorilla Foundation).

Koko's full name is Hanabi-Ko, meaning 'fireworks child' in Japanese. She has appeared on the front cover of many magazines and has even taken part in an internet chat, hosted by AOL. Koko was born in San Francisco Children's Zoo in 1971. She received the first American Sign Language tutorials in the zoo. But at the age of two she was moved to a trailer, where, like Washoe and Chantek, she was brought up like a human child.

On 4 July 2009, Koko's 38th birthday, the Gorilla Foundation sent out a press release stating:

> Koko celebrated her special day with her self-chosen mate, Ndume, and her favourite caregivers. Through conversation she communicated her three birthday wishes.

Koko communicates through ASL, has a vocabulary of more than 1300 words, and understands much more spoken English. Dr. Penny Patterson, co-founder, president and research director of The Gorilla Foundation, chatted with Koko, and she let her know her top three wishes:

1. Koko continues to hope to have a baby of her own, or adopt.
2. Koko looks forward to the day when the Maui Preserve is a reality and she and her family can enjoy the additional space, and a better climate.
3. Koko hopes that people will become aware of the plight of her species before it is too late.

So is it really the case that the great apes language abilities
are comparable with those of human toddlers, let alone being
up to the level indicated above? How much of a breakthrough
did these studies really make in teaching apes a language?

According to the US anthropologist Jane Hill, the results
were extraordinary. She wrote:

> How shall anthropological linguistics assess the significance of
> the recent experiments with apes and language? The question
> is a momentous one. The answer may imply a paradigm shift:
> with Plato finally giving way to Darwin or perhaps 'an identity
> crisis for homo sapiens (Hill, 1978: 89).

She concluded:

> It is unlikely that any of us will in our lifetimes see again a
> scientific breakthrough as profound in its implications as the
> moment when Washoe, the baby chimpanzee, raise her hand
> and signed "come-gimme" to a comprehending human (Hill,
> 1978: 109).

But not everyone was impressed with the apes' achievements,
nor accepted at face value the claims made by those involved
in the ape language projects.

Herbert Terrace opens his 1987 book *Nim: A chimpanzee who
learned sign language* describing the following conversation:

> 'Teacher: *What want you?*
> Student: *Eat more apple.*
> Teacher: *Who want eat more apple?*
> Student: *Me Nim eat more apple.*
> Teacher: *What colour apple?*
> Student: *Apple red.*
> Teacher: *Want you more eat?*
> Student: *Banana, raisin.*'

Terrace states that his book is 'a personal account of a scientific
project whose main goal was to teach an infant chimpanzee
to use sign language' (Terrace, 1987: 4). The student was Nim
Chimpsky at two and a half years of age. Terrace had been

inspired by the Washoe project to investigate the possible language abilities of chimpanzees. As Terrace postulated: 'It is not unreasonable to presume that some precursor of the ability to use language exists in apes' (Terrace, 1987: 5).

Terrace and his colleagues decided to raise Nim like a human child, but to use more rigorous experimental techniques than had been used in the other ape language projects. From two weeks of age Nim was raised in a home environment by human surrogate parents and teachers who communicated with him and with each other using American Sign Language. At first the results of the study did seem to support the idea of a human and ape equivalence in language abilities. As Terrace wrote in an article in *Science* in 1979: 'Superficially many of [Nim's] utterances seem like sentences' (Terrace *et al.*, 1979: 891).

However, he later made a *volte face*, causing a storm among primatologists, and quickly became the *bête noire* of the ape language world. Not only did he question the legitimacy of his own interpretations, and completely re-assess his own data, he re-evaluated data available from other ape language studies. Terrace concluded: 'I could find no evidence of an ape's grammatical competence, either in my data or those of others' (Terrace, 1979: 67). He claimed that: 'Each instance of presumed grammatical competence could be explained adequately by simple nonlinguistic processes' (Terrace *et al.*, 1979: 891).

After analysing hours of video recordings of Nim communicating with a researcher, Terrace concluded:

> An ape signs mainly in response to his teachers' urgings, in order to obtain certain objects or activities. Combinations of signs are not used creatively to generate particular meanings. Instead, they are used for emphasis or in response to the teacher's unwitting demands that the ape produce as many contextually relevant signs as possible (Terrace, 1981: 107–108).

Analysing data over a 17 month period, up until Nim was nearly three years of age, Terrace and his team found 2700 different two or three sign combinations. Because of the large number of sign combinations, they ruled out the possibility that Nim had learned the particular combinations by rote. But neither did they conclude that these utterances resembled sentences. 'Nim's general use of combinations bears only a superficial similarity to a child's early utterances,' the researchers wrote (Terrace *et al.*, 1979: 894).

Terrace and colleagues point out that as the mean length of children's utterances increase so does the complexity of their word combinations. So, for instance, subject-verb and verb-object two-word combinations become subject-verb-object three-word combinations. There was no such order to Nim's three or four sign combinations, which included utterances such as 'banana eat me Nim', 'grape eat Nim eat' and 'eat me Nim drink'.

Interestingly, further analysis of the data between the ages of 26 and 45 months showed no increase in the mean number of signs in Nim's utterances. Also, Nim imitated and interrupted his teacher's utterances much more than a child imitates or interrupts an adult's speech. He had not grasped the give-and-take of conversations in the way young children do. Nor did he tend to creatively come up with new word utterances. So while Nim did learn 125 signs, the researchers found no evidence of the chimp having acquired anything worthy of the name 'language'.

Terrace also analysed films and videotape transcripts of Washoe and Koko, concluding:

> [Their] use of signs suggests a type of interaction between an ape and its trainer that has little to do with human language. In each instance the sole function of the ape's signing appears to be to request various rewards that can be obtained only by signing. Little, if any, evidence is available that an ape signs in order to exchange information with its trainer, as opposed to simply demanding some object or activity (Terrace, 1981: 109–110).

Terrace and his colleagues refer to the widely cited example of Washoe's ability to creatively produce new meanings through combining individual signs. When asked 'what that?' upon seeing a swan in water, Washoe answered 'water bird'. The Gardners had claimed that this was evidence of Washoe being able to use adjectives – with 'water' being used as an adjective to describe what type of bird a swan is. But Terrace argues that there is no basis to concluding that Washoe was characterising the swan as a bird that inhabits water. Instead she may merely have signed the two things she could see when asked 'what that?'. Whether an ape uses particular signs as adjectives 'cannot be decided on the basis of a single anecdote, no matter how compelling that anecdote may seem to an English-speaking observer', they write (Terrace *et al.*, 1979: 896).

An additional criticism of the Washoe project is the extent to which they conflated natural gestures with the signs of American Sign Language. In *Aping Language* Joel Wallman points out that the Washoe team 'improperly treated' a substantial number of natural gestures 'as signs' (Wallman, 1992: 53). 'These natural gestures made up a significant proportion of Washoe's productions and thus inflated measures of the extent of her signing activity', he argued (Wallman 1992: 53).

One ex-volunteer to the post-Washoe project, a deaf American Sign Language user, argued that not only did the team include natural gestures as part of the apes repertoire of 'signs', but 'when the chimp scratched itself they would record it as the sign for *scratch*'. He recounted:

> They kept all kinds of records. The most important was the logbook of signs. Every time the chimp made a sign, we were supposed to write it down in the log ... They were always complaining because my log didn't show enough signs. All the hearing people turned in logs with long lists of signs. They always saw more signs than I did..I watched really carefully. The chimps hands are moving constantly. Maybe I missed something, but I don't think so. I just wasn't seeing any signs. The hearing people were logging every movement the chimp made as a sign. Every time the chimp put his finger in his mouth, they'd say, 'Oh, he's making the sign for *drink*,' and they'd give him some milk (Neisser, 1983: 214–215).

The 'native' ASL user noted that the chimps often 'held up their arms so you could tickle them under the armpits'. One day he found that this movement – 'arms held over head, fingers touching' was recorded as the sign for 'more'. But, as he points out, 'the *more* sign in ASL is not made over the head but in front of the body, and the hands are not just flopping, they have a definite shape' (Neisser, 1983: 216).

In *The Language Instinct,* evolutionary psychologist Steven Pinker concludes that the 'preposterous claim' that the apes learnt American Sign Language 'is based on the myth that ASL is a crude system of pantomimes and gestures rather than a full language with complex phonology, morphology, and syntax' (Pinker, 1994: 337).

Commenting on the impending internet chat with Koko the gorilla, Katherine Borsecnik, vice president of network programming for AOL, said: 'This event is providing a once in a lifetime opportunity for millions of AOL members to tap into the knowledge and compassion these foundations and Koko have for saving endangered species', (The Gorillla Foundation, News).

But how enlightening was the chat with Koko? For *Time* magazine the event quickly devolved into a 'Dada exercise' and Koko's teacher, Francine Patterson, used 'some pretty impressive logic to expand her simian friend's limited communication skills' (*Time,* 11 May 1998). *Time* illustrated the point with a partial transcript (*Time,* 11 May 1998):

Q: Koko are you going to have a baby in the future?
Koko: Pink.
Patterson: We had earlier discussion about colours today.
Q: Do you like to chat with people?
Koko: Fine nipple.
Patterson: Nipple rhymes with people, she doesn't sign people per se, she was trying to do a 'sounds like ...'
Q: Does she have hair? Or is it like fur?
Koko: Fine.
Patterson: She has fine hair.
Q: Koko, do you feel love from the humans who have raised you?
Koko: Lips, apple give me.
Patterson: People give her her favourite foods.
Koko: Koko loves that nipple drink, go.
Patterson: She's kissing her alligator.
Koko: Fake.

Q: What does fake mean to her?
Koko: Gorilla.

Steven Pinker similarly believes that far too much has been made of apes' language abilities, and he directs much of his fire at Patterson. He writes in *The Language Instinct*:

> Patterson in particular has found ways to excuse Koko's performance on the grounds that the gorilla is fond of puns, jokes, metaphors, and mischievous lies. Generally the stronger the claims made about the animals abilities, the skimpier the data made available to the scientific community for evaluation (Pinker, 1994: 337).

He stresses that we all have a tendency to anthropomorphise – thinking that animals are capable of a lot more than they are in reality. 'People who spend a lot of time with animals are prone to developing indulgent attitudes about their powers of communication' he writes, giving the example of his great-aunt Bella who 'insisted in all sincerity that her Siamese cat Rusty understood English' (Pinker, 1994: 337). But we should expect more of those involved in ape language studies. They should be prepared to critically evaluate the data from their studies. Instead, many of the claims of those involved in ape language studies are not much more scientific than those of his great-aunt, Pinker argues.

Joel Wallman is also sceptical. In his book *Aping Language* he provides a detailed analysis of the experimental methods and conclusions of the various ape-language projects, concluding:

> None of the ape-language projects succeeded, despite employing years of tutelage far more intense than that experienced by most children, in implanting in an ape a capacity for language equal to that of a young child, let alone an adult (Wallman, 1992: 4).

And the husband and wife team Thomas Sebeok, a linguist, and Jean Umiker-Sebeok, an anthropologist, have raised doubts about the ape language claims, arguing that investigators and experimenters unwittingly convince themselves that the apes' reactions are more humanlike than the evidence suggests, because they start by interpreting apes' behaviour as if it were human. They write:

> Time and again researchers read anomalous chimpanzee and gorilla signs as jokes, insults, metaphors, and the like. In one case, an animal was reported to be deliberately joking when, in response to persistent attempts to get it to sign 'drink' (by tilting its hand at its mouth), it made the sign perfectly, but at its ear rather than its mouth (Sebeok & Umiker-Sebeok, 1979: 81).

Much has been made of Kanzi's communication skills, but as Wallman points out Kanzi's 25 most frequent two-item and 25 most frequent three-item combinations are all requests for something. Also, 'no evidence is presented for grammatical patterning in these combinations, presumably because none exists', he writes (Wallman, 1992:95)

Referring to Kanzi's 'sentences', Mithen notes:

> They are not good sentences. In fact they are awful, whether compared with those of William Shakespeare or any three-year-old child. Savage-Rumbaugh and her colleagues acknowledge that Kanzi's range of vocabulary and use of grammatical rules is not as advanced as that of a three-year old. But they do not recognise the yawning gulf that in fact exists (Mithen, 1996: 95).

Unlike ape communications which are almost exclusively requests for things, three-year-old human children use language for many purposes, including just to comment on the world around them. Despite years of intensive training, the average length of the apes' multi-sign utterances remained relatively constant. But, as Pinker points out: 'With nothing more than exposure to speakers, the average length of a child's sentences shoots off like a rocket.' (Pinker, 1994: 339). Children's sentences increase in length and complexity with age. By three years of age they can string together sentences of 10 words or more.

Pinker writes:

If we divide language development into somewhat arbitrary stages, like Syllable Babbling, Gibberish Babbling, One–Word Utterances, and Two-Word Strings, the next stage would have to be called All Hell Breaks Loose (Pinker, 1994: 269).

In the 1960s the psychologist Roger Brown carried out ground-breaking analyses of children's language development. Armed with a portable tape-recorder Brown's team of researchers recorded the speech of three young children – 'Adam', 'Eve' and 'Sarah' – as they acquired language. They gathered a wealth of data and set about analysing the children's speech to account for both the length and complexity of their utterances (Brown, 1973).

Transcripts of Adam's speech between the ages of two and three years of age show the extent to which language flourishes in these early years. At two years of age Adam was producing a large number of word combinations, the majority of which were two-word combinations. He also produced some three word, and, albeit very rarely, four word combinations at this early age. Examples of his word combinations at two years of age included 'Hear tractor', 'Adam make tower' and 'See truck, mommy'.

By the time Adam was two years and five months his sentences often consisted of four word combinations, such as 'Mommy talking bout lady' and 'Now put boots on'. By three years of age his sentences had increased to six word combinations or more, such as 'I going wear that to wedding' and 'You dress me up like a baby elephant'. Two months later his sentences consisted of more than ten words, such as 'When it's got a flat tire it's need a go to the station', or 'Can I keep the screwdriver just like a carpenter keep the screwdriver?'

Eve's language was more advanced than Adam's. She was speaking in sentences before the age of two, saying things like: 'I sit in my high chair yesterday' and 'Sue making more coffee for Fraser'. Of course, there are grammatical errors in all these sentences, but compare these sentences to Nim': 'Give orange me give eat orange me eat orange give me eat orange give me you' (Terrace, 1979: 895).

Moreover, as Robbins Burling points out, language is not only a way to communicate. He writes:

It has also become a tool that helps us think clearly. As language
has developed the human mind has been transformed (Burling,
2005: 17).

The Russian psychologist Lev Vygotsky showed that a significant moment in the development of the human individual
occurs when language and practical intelligence converge
(Vygotsky, 1986). It is when thought and speech come together
that children's thinking is raised to new heights and they start
acquiring truly human characteristics. Language becomes a
tool of thought, allowing children increasingly to master their
own behaviour.

As Vygotsky pointed out, young children will often talk
out loud – to themselves it seems – particularly when they
are carrying out fairly challenging tasks, such as a jigsaw
puzzle or a construction task. This 'egocentric speech' does
not disappear, but gradually becomes internalised into private
inner speech – also known as thought. So children are using
speech to guide their actions, in the way adults use thought
– or what Vygotsky calls 'internal speech' – to guide theirs.
Vygotsky and fellow psychologist Alexander Romanovich Luria
concluded that 'the meeting between speech and thinking is
a major event in the development of the individual; in fact, it
is this connection that raises human thinking to extraordinary
heights' (Luria & Vygotsky, 1992: 140). Apes never develop the
ability to use language to regulate their own actions.

Ape communications cannot therefore be elevated to the
status of human language. Human beings use speech to
guide our actions. We debate and discuss ideas, construct
arguments – drawing on past experiences and imagining
future possibilities – in order to change the opinions of others.
Apes do not.

Chapter Six
Evolution and Consciousness

'When we group chimpanzees together with, say, snakes, as "animals," we imply that the gap between us and chimpanzees is greater than the gap between chimpanzees and snakes. But in evolutionary terms this is nonsense. Chimpanzees and bonobos are our closest relatives, and we humans, not gorillas or orangutans, are their closest relatives.'

Peter Singer, Great Ape Project: Equality beyond humanity,
Fourth Estate, London, 1993.

When I started writing *Just Another Ape?*, I anticipated that by studying and analysing ape behaviour, and apes' performance on technical and social intelligence tasks, we could gain some insight into the evolutionary emergence of our unique abilities. After all, we split from a common ancestor with chimpanzees only six million years ago, which is not a very long time in evolutionary terms. We share more than 98 percent of our genetic make-up with chimpanzees, which is about the same amount of genetic relatedness as horses and zebras or rats and mice. One might therefore assume that apes resemble us in more ways than just our physiology and our looks, and may share some of our unique abilities, albeit in an embryonic form.

Therefore, investigations into the behaviour and abilities of apes might give us some insight into our evolutionary past, several million years back, and arguably could help us start answering the difficult question of how the human mind and human culture emerged tens of thousands of years ago. Having investigated further, however, I am no longer convinced that the study of apes can help explain much about human behaviour, for reasons I'll go on to explain.

In earlier chapters I have argued that human beings have something that no other animal has: an ability to participate in a collective cognition. Because we, as individuals, are able to draw on the collective knowledge of humanity – in a way no other animal can draw on the achievements of their conspecifics or of previous generations – our individual abilities go way beyond what evolution has endowed us with. Our species is no longer constrained by our biology.

In *A Mind So Rare* Merlin Donald, professor of psychology at Queen's University in Ontario writes:

> The key to understanding the human intellect is not so much the design of the individual brain as the synergy of many brains. We have evolved an adaptation for living in culture, and our exceptional powers as a species derive from the curious fact that we have broken out of one of the most critical limitations of traditional nervous systems – their loneliness, or solipsism (Donald, 2002: xiii).

Donald is not arguing that there is such a thing as a 'group mind'. 'Our minds are still very much sealed into their biological containers. But they can do remarkably little on their own. They depend on culture for virtually everything that is unique to the human world, including our basic communicative and thought skills' (Donald, 2002: xiv)

It may be hard to understand how something as elusive as an ability to participate in a collective culture emerged in the course of evolution. But it did.

Many scientists reject any notion that human beings have abilities that are profoundly different from other animals. To do so, some scientists seem to fear, will give ammunition to creationists and spiritualists. Science editor of the *Daily Mail*, Michael Hanlon, argues that it is not possible that human beings are unique among the animal kingdom. He writes:

> That the brains of mammals, reptiles, birds, amphibians and even fish share common structures and genetic backgrounds suggests quite strongly that our self-awareness is almost

certainly not unique. Because not to draw this conclusion would be to assume something very strange indeed, something along the Cartesian lines – that somehow, at some point in the evolution of *Homo sapiens,* and *Homo sapiens* alone, something magical invaded our skulls in the Pleistocene and set up home (Hanlon, 2007: 36).

But, we do not need to turn to spiritual or 'magical' explanations in order to understand that the difference between human beings and other animals is fundamental rather than one of degrees. There are some fascinating theories put forward in the last decade that go quite far in explaining the emergence, through evolution, of uniquely powerful human abilities. We don't know how or when, but there must have been some gene mutation or set of mutations tens of thousands of years ago that endowed us with the unique ability to participate in a collective cognition.

There must be a genetic basis to our uniqueness. Otherwise we would be able to raise chimps, bonobos, gorillas and orang-utans as humans and in the process make them human. But despite the dedication of a number of primatologists, the cognitive and linguistic abilities of the great apes have never surpassed those of a one or two-year-old child. This is because apes clearly lack the precondition for becoming human: a human genetic make-up.

There are very many unanswered questions with regards to what past accidents and climatic changes played a role in creating the biological basis for the emergence of our unique abilities. But, to reiterate, even if we did have all the answers to how and why our human genetic make-up evolved, we would not – as a result of these insights – be able to explain why we behave the way we do today. The evolution of the human genetic make-up is merely the *precondition* for the emergence of distinctly human cultural abilities. We need to look to cultural evolution, rather than genetic evolution, to explain the vast gulf that exists between the capabilities and achievements of humans and those of apes.

So what do we know about human evolution? The answer is: a lot more than we did just a few decades ago, but very many pieces of the jigsaw puzzle are still missing and may never be found. The leading cognitive archaeologist Steven Mithen writes in *The Prehistory of the Mind: A search for the origins of art, religion and science:*

> During the final 2.5 million years of [human evolution], our ancestors left traces of their behaviour such as their stone tools, food debris and paintings on cave walls. They only left written records towards the very end of this period, starting a mere 5,000 years ago (Mithen, 1998: 1).

Despite relying only on 'traces' of our ancestors behaviour, one thing we do know for sure is that the human lineage has undergone 'radical changes' in the last few million years (Povinelli, 2004). Daniel Povinelli, director of the Cognitive Evolution Group at the University of Louisiana at Lafayette, argues that this is in stark contrast to chimpanzees, which have in all likelihood changed very little in the six million years since we 'split' from our common ancestor. He writes:

> Since this split, humans have re-sculpted their bodies from head to toe: quite literally, in fact. As our lineage became bipedal, the pelvis, the knee, and the foot, were all drastically re-shaped, with modifications in the hand (including new muscles) soon following. To top it all off, we ultimately tripled the size of our brain, probably focusing disproportionately on the seat of higher cognitive function: the prefrontal cortex. Oh yes, and at some point during all of this (no one knows exactly when), natural language – perhaps the most noticeable of our adaptations – emerged as well (Povinelli, 2004: 30).

The emergence of language undoubtedly played a central role in the emergence of human consciousness. In *The Talking Ape*, Robbins Burling argues that language should be given a good deal of credit for turning us into 'a most peculiar animal'. He writes:

> Language changed the way we use our minds and it prepared us for the literate, urban, and technological society that our ancestors began to build about six thousand years ago (Burling, 2005: 210).

Friedrich Engels argued in *The Part Played by Labour in the Transition from Ape to Man* that tool-use – or labour – 'created man himself'. He wrote:

> Mastery over nature began with the development of the hand, with labour, and widened man's horizon at every new advance. He was continually discovering new, hitherto unknown, properties of objects. On the other hand, the development of labour necessarily helped to bring the members of society closer together by increasing cases of mutual support and joint activity. In short, men in the making arrived at the point where *they had something to say* to each other (Engels, 1982: 5–6).

Despite writing at a time when very little was known about our evolutionary past, Engels identified two driving forces that must have played a key part in bringing about the transformation of our ancestors: labour, or tool-use, and language. He wrote: 'First labour, after it and then with it speech – these were the two essential stimuli under the influence of which the brain of the ape gradually changed into that of man' (Engels, 1982: 6–7). While we now know that it was not as simple as a transformation of the brain from ape to man, these forces are undoubtedly part of the story, and the notion that they had a role in *making* man, rather than simply being components of human nature, was particularly insightful, as we shall see.

We know now that there were two major spurts in brain size in our evolutionary past – one around 1.8 million years ago with the appearance of *Homo erectus* and one between 500,000 and 200,000 years ago, before the arrival of *Homo sapiens sapiens*.

Many archaeologists and palaeontologist link the first spurt in brain size with novel tool-making abilities. 'Sometime about a million and a half years ago, some forgotten genius of the hominid world did an unexpected thing. He (or possibly she) took one stone and carefully used it to shape another. The result was a simple teardrop-shaped hand-axe, but it was the worlds first piece of advanced technology', the best-selling American author Bill Bryson writes in *A Short History of Nearly Everything* (Bryson, 2004).

Scientists have still not found any solid evidence of a transformation in the behaviour of our ancestors that corresponds with the second spurt in brain size. As Steven Mithen writes:

> The two really dramatic transformations in human behaviour occurred long after the modern size of the brain had evolved. They are both associated exclusively with *Homo sapiens sapiens*. The first was the cultural explosion between 60,000 and 30,000 years ago, when the first art, complex technology and religion appeared. The second was the rise of farming 10,000 years ago, when people for the first time began to plant crops and domesticate animals (Mithen, 1996: 8).

Nobody knows for certain how our unique capabilities emerged. But one thing that is clear is that the emergence of our unique human abilities are the result of innumerable climatic and geographical changes, and 'accidents', in our distant and not so distant evolutionary past. There was nothing inevitable, or 'teleological' about it. And it would be meaningless to isolate *one* determining event, because each change is reliant on previous changes. If it were not for the events that led to the extinction of the dinosaurs 65 million years ago, maybe the first anthropoids – that is, apes and monkeys – wouldn't have emerged 50 million years ago. If it were not for the dramatic fall in global temperatures and humidity around six million years ago, maybe the upright posture of our ancestors and bipedalism would never have emerged. If it were not for another period of global cooling approximately two million years ago maybe there would not have been a rapid expansions in hominids' brain size 1.8 million years ago.

A period of global cooling between seven and five million years ago, leading to a particularly bad drought in East Africa, and with it changes in vegetation, may have spurred the emergence of the first hominids. It is likely that our ancestors began to walk upright because of environmental changes - in particular, the growth of open spaces and, as a result, changes in the distribution of food. According to paleoanthropologist Brian Richmond, lead author in a review article on the origins of human bipedalism:

Such climatic intervals would involve expansion of open environments. In near-equatorial areas of Africa, forests would fragment during these intervals, producing mosaics of dense forest, closed and open woodlands, and grasslands (Richmond, 2001).

These changes to their habitat resulted in some maintaining 'a forest-oriented adaptation', while others 'may have begun to exploit forest margins and grassy woodlands' (Richmond, 2001).

One of the earliest pieces of evidence of early hominids is a 3.2 million year old partial skeleton of the humanlike creature Lucy found in Ethiopia in 1974. Lucy was named after the Beatles' song *'Lucy in the Sky with Diamonds'* which was playing on the radio when the man who made the discovery, American anthropologist Donald Johanson, was celebrating with his team back at camp. It was later concluded that Lucy was a female member of the species *Australopithecus afarensis*, which first appeared in Africa about four million years ago. The brain size of Lucy was most likely equivalent to that of today's chimpanzees, and she had many anatomical features in common with apes. However, her distinguishing feature was that – like humans – she walked upright.

Spencer Wells, former head of the population genetics research group at Oxford's Wellcome Trust Centre for Human Genetics, describes aspects of the journey from ape to man:

> Over time, these upright apes became completely bipedal, allowing them to see further and run faster, while leaving the hands free to do other things...which they started to do in earnest around 2m years ago when we see the first evidence of tool use by our ancestors (Wells, 3 July 2003).

There are not many fossil remains of the first species of the *Homo* lineage – *Homo habilis* – that emerged around 2.5 million years ago. *Homo habilis*, meaning 'handy man', with reference to the species' supposed tool making abilities, had a slightly larger brain than the *Australopithecines*, but their brains were still less than half the size of modern *Homo sapiens*.

Steven Mithen points out that although the function of the stone tools from this period remains unclear, 'there is little doubt that some were made to make other tools – such as the production of stone flake to sharpen a stick' (Mithen, 1996: 106). The making of tools to make another tools is something of which apes have shown no evidence of being capable.

With the emergence of *Homo Erectus*, around 1.8 million years ago, there was a spurt in brain size and evidence of new types of stone tools, such as hand-axes. This is the first hominid to have moved out of its East African evolutionary environment. As Spencer Wells points out '[*Homo Erectus*] even seems to have wandered out of Africa around 1.8m years ago – Java Man and Peking Man were both part of the *Homo Erectus* family. He didn't stray far from the tropics though (particularly when the world cooled down during the periodic ice ages)' (Wells, 3 July 2003).

The brain size of *Homo erectus* remained relatively stable until 500,000 years ago with another period of rapid expansion lasting 300,000 years. Curiously, as I pointed out earlier, this expansion in brain size does not seem to correspond with any dramatic changes in tool-using and tool-making abilities. Although there is evidence of some novel tool-making abilities of *Homo sapiens sapiens* around 100,000 years ago – such as the making of bone artefacts and the placing of animal parts into human burials – as Mithen writes, 'other than these glimpses of something new, the props of *Homo sapiens sapiens* are almost identical to those of Early Humans' (Mithen: 1998: 171). The 'major turning point in prehistory', Mithen explains, only occurred after *Homo sapiens sapiens* had been on the stage for some tens of thousands of years.

According to evolutionary biologist Jared Diamond, for most of the millions of years since our lineage diverged from that of our common ape ancestors, we remained little more than glorified chimpanzees in how we made our living. 'Human history at last took off 50,000 years ago, at the time of what I have termed our Great Leap Forward', Diamond writes in his Pulitzer Prize-winning book *Guns, Germs, and Steel* (Diamond, 1988: 39). This Palaeolithic revolution was marked by the appearance of far more sophisticated tools, more developed hunting techniques, oceanic travel, cave drawings, ceremonial burials and much more. Diamond writes: 'Tools were produced in diverse and distinctive shapes so modern that their functions as needles, awls, engraving tools, and so on are obvious to us'(Diamond, 1988: 39).

Similarly evolutionary psychologist Richard Byrne writes: '[T]here is no doubt that at the Upper Palaeolithic, a completely different level of sophistication suddenly emerges. Before these anatomically modern humans of the Upper Palaeolithic, stone tools could all have been produced by animals with little more cognitive sophistication in tool-making than chimpanzees.' (Byrne, 2006: 190).

Anthropologist Marvin Harris describes this period as one of 'cultural take-off' linked to 'linguistic take-off', when the rate of change and the complexity of human culture increases by 'many orders of magnitude' despite no apparent increase in brain size. Cultural take-off is linked to the 'uniquely human capacity for language and for language-assisted systems of thought', he argues (Harris, 1988: 138).

Evolution must have endowed our ancestors with something uniquely powerful: something that came into force around 50,000 years ago and in the process transformed their social and technical intelligence. As Tomasello points out in *The Cultural Origins of Human Cognition*:

> The fact is, there simply has not been enough time for normal processes of biological evolution involving genetic variation and natural selection to have created, one by one, each of the cognitive skills necessary for humans to invent and maintain complex tool-use industries and technologies, complex forms of symbolic communication and representation, and complex social organisations and institutions. And the puzzle is only magnified if we take seriously current research in paleoanthropology suggesting that (a) for all but the last 2 million years the human lineage showed no sign of anything other than typical great ape cognitive skills, and (b) the first dramatic signs of species-unique cognitive skills emerged only in the last one-quarter of a million years with modern *Homo sapiens* (Tomasello, 1999: 3–4).

Crucially, this means it was not 'apes' who suddenly became human, but ape-like humans who began to behave very differently. Because of the marked differences between the abilities of apes and the abilities *of Homo sapiens sapiens* from the period of this 'great leap forward', I am no longer sure that ape studies can tell us very much at all about how the biological precondition for our uniqueness emerged. The key challenge is instead to understand this period of cultural take-off. We need to try to explain what could have caused this explosion in creativity. The Palaeolithic revolution did not correspond with an increase in brain size. So brain capacity alone cannot explain this sudden leap forward.

Mithen explains the cultural explosion of the Middle/Upper Palaeolithic transition on the basis of 'changes in the nature of language and consciousness within the mind': 'once Early Humans started talking, they just couldn't stop', he writes (Mithen: 1998: 211). Mithen argues that the language of Early Humans was a 'social language' – 'they used language as a means to send and receive social information', that is to establish pecking orders, loyalties and reciprocal expectations, rather than information about subjects such as tool-use or hunting. With larger group sizes, language may have allowed Early Humans to build social ties more effectively than grooming, the staple form of sociability for apes. By 250,000 years ago this was 'a language with an extensive lexicon and grammatical complexity', he writes (Mithen 1998: 211). This 'social language' at some point became transformed into the 'general-purpose' language we use today, Mithen argues.

Only when language started acting as a vehicle for delivering information about the world other than the social world, could individuals start thinking about their non-social thought-processes and knowledge, Mithen argues. 'As a result, the whole of human behaviour was pervaded with the flexibility and creativity that is characteristic of Modern Humans' (Mithen, 1998: 219)

This period is characterised by a whole series of 'cultural sparks' that occurred at different times in different parts of the world, Mithen explains, but 'it is perhaps only after 30,000 years ago that we can be confident that the hectic pace of cultural change had begun in earnest throughout the globe' (Mithen, 1998: 173). This is when the first cave paintings and personal decorations such as beads and pendants were created.

Michael Tomasello puts forward a different, equally well-argued hypothesis. He argues that there is only one possible solution to the puzzle: the only biological mechanism that could bring about these kinds of changes in such a short period of time is a new capacity for 'social or cultural transmission, which works on time scales many orders of magnitude faster than those of organic evolution' (Tomasello, 1999: 4). By social or cultural transmission, Tomasello is referring to a powerful ability to learn from our fellows. He writes:

> This scenario solves our time problem because it posits one and only one biological adaptation – which could have happened at any time in human evolution, including quite recently (Tomasello, 1999: 7).

Tomasello explains that a more simple form of this kind of learning is a fairly common evolutionary process 'that enables individual organisms to save much time and effort, not to mention risk, by exploiting the already existing knowledge and skills of conspecifics' (Tomasello, 1999: 4). Examples include rat pups only eating the food that their mothers eat, or young birds learning their species-typical song by mimicking their parents. For human beings this more simple ability to learn from our fellows must have at some stage in our evolutionary past been transformed into something a lot more powerful. As I showed in Chapter Four, the human form of social learning is qualitatively different from other animals' social learning, in that human beings are able to think about unobservable forces such as intentions, goals and desires. This ability seems to have emerged out of an innate desire to engage with others about the world around us.

Josep Call and Michael Tomasello write in *The Gestural Communication of Apes and Monkeys*:

> Much more than other primates, human beings seem motivated to engage with one another in collaborative activites involving shared goals, and to share experience with one another simply for the sake of doing it (Call & Tomasello, 2007: 229).

A similar argument is put forward by Jennifer Vonk and Daniel Povinelli at the University of Louisiana at Lafayette.

They argue that the key difference between humans and nonhumans is that we can reason about unobservable events and forces, and other animals cannot. Evolution has 'sculpted the minds' of nearly all social species to detect and respond to observable behaviour, but 'the ability to explain behaviours in terms of unobservable mental states is an innovation peculiar to humans'. Vonk and Povinelli propose that this special ability may have been 'grafted into existing cognitive systems for reasoning about social behaviour that they inherited from their ancestor with the African apes' (Vonk & Povinelli, 2006: 27).

How exactly it came about we may never know. But at some stage in our evolutionary past we lacked this ability, and now we have it. British psychologist and broadcaster Nicholas Humphrey provides a fitting description of these two stages in an article in the *New Scientist* back in 1982:

> So, once upon a time there were animals ancestral to man who were not conscious. That is not to say that these animals lacked brains. They were no doubt percipient, intelligent, complexly motivated creatures, whose internal control mechanisms were in many respects the equals of our own. But it is to say that they had no way of looking in upon the mechanism. They had clever brains, but blank minds. Their brains would receive and process information from their sense organs without their minds being conscious of any accompanying sensation; their brains would be moved by, say, hunger or fear without their minds being conscious of any accompanying emotion; their brains would undertake voluntary actions without their minds being conscious of any accompanying volition ... And so these ancestral animals went about their lives, deeply ignorant of an inner explanation for their own behaviour (Humphrey, 1982: 475).

Humphrey explains that it is very difficult for us to get our heads around the idea that there can be ways of learning and behaving that do not involve any awareness of inner states. He writes:

> To our way of thinking such ignorance has to be strange. We have experienced so often the connection between conscious feelings and behaviour, grown so used to the notion that our feelings

are the causes of our actions, that it is hard to imagine that in the absence of feelings behaviour could carry on at all. It is true that in rare cases human beings may show a quite unexpected competence to do things without being conscious of their inner reasons: the case, for example, of 'blind-sight', where a patient with damaged visual centres in the brain can point to a light without being conscious of any sensation accompanying his seeing (and without, as he says, knowing how he does it). But the patient himself in such a case confesses himself baffled; and you and I will not pretend that that would not be our reaction too (Humphrey, 1982: 475).

As Tomasello explains, the cultural processes that this one adaptation unleashed – a powerful ability to teach and learn from our fellows – did not then create new cognitive skills out of nothing. Instead this one adaptation took existing individually based cognitive skills – such as those possessed by most primates for dealing with space, objects, tools, quantities, categories, social relationships, communication and social learning – and transformed them into new, culturally based cognitive skills with a social-collective dimension' (Tomasello, 1999: 7).

This ability to learn from each other would have meant that the skills, discoveries and innovations of the most intelligent group members were quickly passed on to other group members. Each new generation would learn from the insights gained by previous generations and would be able to build upon those insights.

A colleague of Tomasello's at the Max Planck Institute for Evolutionary Anthropology in Germany, Esther Herrmann, similarly argues that our unique abilities are due to a 'species-specific set of cognitive skills' for participating and exchanging knowledge in cultural groups that emerge 'early in ontogeny', that is, early in the individual's life span (Herrmann *et al.*, 2008: 1360). She argues that human adults possess distinctive cognitive skills as a result of 'children's early emerging, specialised skills for absorbing accumulated skilful practices and knowledge of their social group (so that a child growing up outside any human culture would develop few distinctive human cognitive skills)' (Herrmann *et al.*, 2008: 1361).

These social cognitive skills may have evolved as a result of the advantages of more complex forms of collaborative activity – such as hunting – that required more sophisticated means of communication and social learning. Selection pressures in our distant evolutionary past may therefore have honed our social learning processes.

This ability to engage in a collective culture led to a cultural explosion tens of thousands of years ago, with the result that human lives are incomparable to those of our ape-like ancestors. While apes are still struggling to crack open nuts, humans have made life-changing inventions such as the internal combustion engine, the harnessing of electricity, the creation of life-saving vaccines and x-rays and much more. While apes are still struggling to communicate in the here-and-now, humans have invented alphabets and other forms of written symbols and ever more impressive means to disseminate the written word – from the invention of paper and ink to the typewriter and the internet. While apes are living in similar-sized groups as they did several million years ago, human beings have created cities, nation states, governments and global economic institutions.

Conclusion
Celebrating the Achievements of Humanity

'The cuddlesome "chimps are us" image is as misguided, wrong and morally and intellectually bankrupt as the infamous PG Tips Tea advertisements that ran for 40 years on British television'

Jeremy Taylor, Not a Chimp: The hunt for genes that make us human, *Oxford University Press, Oxford, 2009.*

In the animal rights activists' 'bible', *Animal Liberation (1975),* the father of the animal rights movement Peter Singer describes the 'routine torture' and 'abuse' of millions of animals in farming and in the name of scientific research. The way human beings treat animals is morally wrong, he argues, because like us animals are 'beings with interests' – that is, beings that are capable of feeling pleasure or pain. Singer builds on the work of the 19th Century utilitarian philosopher Jeremy Bentham who famously wrote: 'The question is not, Can they reason? nor Can they talk? but, Can they suffer?'

Singer writes:

> At a minimum, a sentient animal has an interest in a painless, pleasurable life. And if he or she possesses this interest, then he or she deserves no less consideration of his or her interests than we give to our own (Singer, 2006: 19).

There is nothing special about human beings in Singer's eyes. There is no clear dividing line between us and other animals. So there is no justification for treating animals differently from humans. In *Animal Rights and Human Obligations,* Singer writes:

> Once we ask why it should be that all humans - including infants, mental defectives, psychopaths, Hitler, Stalin and the rest – have some kind of dignity or worth that no elephant, pig, or chimpanzee can ever achieve, we see that this question is as difficult to answer as our original request for some relevant fact that justifies the inequality of humans and other animals (Singer, 1976).

Similarly, Michael Hanlon argues in his recent book *Ten Questions Science Can't Answer (Yet!)* that the science of animal cognition has undergone a 'revolution' in the last three decades, with the new findings all suggesting animals have more complex and sophisticated mental lives than we thought. He writes:

> Not only are animals cleverer than we once believed, they are probably also more emotional, more self-aware and in many ways more like us than we ever believed. Here, science is on a collision course with the world of accepted ethics and morality, and in the near future it is easy to see a revolution occurring thanks to what we are learning (Hanlon, 2007: 20).

He warns that by unlocking the 'secret mental life of the beasts' we will open 'a very nasty can of worms', because of the status animals are given in today's society (Hanlon, 2007: 20).

For Singer the answer is fairly straightforward: when deciding whether something is morally wrong or not we need to take into account all 'beings with interest', he argues.

It is hard to imagine how we could make any decision in life if we were to follow this advice, as there would be a never-ending list of beings whose interests we would need to consider. However, not to do so, Singer argues, is 'speciesist': To make decisions on the basis of what species a being happens to belong to is the same as endorsing prejudice against particular races or sexes.

The special moral significance given to human beings has historically been on the basis of 'the ability to reason, self-awareness, possessing a sense of justice, language, autonomy, and so on', says Singer. But, he asks, seeming to believe that he has boxed humanists into a corner, how can 'speciesists account for the fact that some human beings are entirely lacking in these characteristics? And what about the evidence for some non-human animals possessing at least some of the advanced cognitive characteristics of humans?

Setting aside the fact that there is no convincing evidence that any animal – not even the great apes – have any of the advances of cognitive capacities of humans, Singer is wrong to conclude that infants and neurologically impaired individuals are somehow less than human. It is not logically inconsistent to identify the ability to participate in our collective culture as the defining human characteristic while avoiding using that same criterion to decide whether or not an individual is human.

The question of when life begins, or questions about the value of life, cannot be reduced to whether an individual has the capacity for social learning and cooperation - if that was the case, then most children under one would not be seen as human. Neither is this something that can be answered biologically. When life begins is a complex social question, defined differently in different societies in different historical periods. So the distinction we make today between a foetus and a neonate is a social, moral and legal one that cannot be justified in terms of cognitive abilities or biology. The physical event of birth does not transform a foetus into a self-aware person. Yet in most societies today a child, once born, is recognised in law as a legal person.

It is a sign of a civilised human society that, even if severely disabled, an individual can be included in our common humanity. The value of human life – and complex questions about life and death – cannot be reduced to a tick-list of capabilities. As Oscar Wilde might have said, that would be the outlook of a cynic: someone who 'knows the price of everything and the value of nothing'.

As I have argued, what it means to be human is the outcome of a complex interplay of evolution, social development and individual life-experiences. We are biological beings like other animals, but we are also fundamentally different from other animals. Our biological instincts are transformed into something qualitatively different through our engagement with society.

In *Civilisation and its Discontents*, the father of psychoanalysis Sigmund Freud, tried to grapple with the relationship between biology and society. He devoted much of his energy in the latter part of his life to understanding the tensions between natural human drives and civilised society. Although Freud vastly overestimated the role of sexuality, he was right to stress that civilised society forces us to subordinate our individual drives and interests to the interests of society as a whole. We cannot, like other animals, operate purely on the basis of maximising our own self-interest.

But Freud did not regard society – or civilisation – in the same bean-counting way as utilitarians like Singer do. Society is not merely a sum of its parts. And civilisation is not merely a force that manages or suppresses the needs and desires of its individual members. Instead civilisation gives individuals a unique pleasure: it plays an important role in creating the conditions for happiness, Freud argued.

In an introduction to *Civilisation and its Discontents*, literary theorist Leo Bersani shows that the exploration of the tensions between the claims of the individual and those of civilisation were 'impressively elaborated' in the work of the German sociologist Georg Simmel – but in 'more measured, less melodramatic terms' than in Freud's writings (Freud, 2002). In Simmel's 1910 essay *The Sociology of Sociability*, he wrote:

> The great problems placed before [the forces of society] are that the individual has to fit himself into a whole system and live for it: that, however, out of this system values and enhancement must flow back to him, that the life of the individual is but a means for the ends of the whole, the life of the whole but an instrument for the purposes of the individual (Simmel, 1971: 137).

Similarly, Merlin Donald writes in *A Mind So Rare*:

> The ultimate irony of human existence is that we are supreme individualists, whose individualism depends almost entirely on culture for its realisation. It came at the price of giving up

the isolationism, or cognitive solipsism, of all other species and entering into a collectivity of mind (Donald, 2002: 12).

Human beings are unique in that we have created culture – or civilisation – and in the process have made ourselves. If we lose sight of our unique capacities we will lose the power to improve our condition and further develop humanity. The main challenge we face today is therefore to uphold a human-centred morality, restoring confidence in the capacity of humans to change society for the better. That means appreciating what we have achieved to date.

I am not arguing that human beings are naturally all good: human history is undeniably full of evidence of human destructiveness. Dolan Cummings, co-founder of the radical humanist campaign group the Manifesto Club, argues on *spiked* that humanists do need to recognise the undeniable fact of human imperfection, insisting that 'it is those of us most committed to social and moral progress who must take this most seriously, look into the depravity in our own hearts, even, and not repent but resolve to go on'. He continues:

> Those of us who believe humans are evolved beings rather than created ones ought to have no problem acknowledging this 'depravity' without getting hung up on it. [...] we are not nearly as good as we wish we were. And if we were never in fact 'meant' to be civilised, perhaps we should not be surprised that it doesn't come naturally, or lose heart because of it (Cummings, 2009).

Human beings are not perfect and never will be, but we are special and unique among the animal kingdom. As sociologist Frank Furedi argues in *Debating Humanism*: 'most important of all we need to understand that whatever the mistakes that we have made we can extract from them lessons that can guide us to move forward (Furedi, 2006: 29).

Those who continually denigrate humans – by blurring the distinction between humans and other animals, and not being prepared to put the case first and foremost for human interests – undermine our ability to change the world for the better.

To me, it is ironic that we, who have something that no other organism has – the ability to evaluate who we are, where we come from and where we are going, and, with that, our place in nature increasingly seem to use this unique ability to downplay our own capacities and achievements. Unless we hold on to the belief in our exceptional abilities we will never be able to envision or build a better future – in which case, we might as well be monkeys.

Bibliography

Adams, D., (1993), 'Meeting a Gorilla' in P. Cavalieri and P. Singer (eds.), *The Great Ape Project*, (London: Fourth Estate).

American Association for the Advancement of Science, (6 September 2007), 'Higher social skills are distinctly human, toddler and ape study reveals', *Science Press Package*, Online. Available HTTP: <http://www.eurekalert.org/features/kids/2007-09/aaft-hss083107. php> (accessed 29 October, 2008).

Bahra, P., (14 April 2009), 'David Attenborough to be patron of Optimum Population Trust', *The Times*. Online. Available HTTP: <http://www.timesonline.co.uk/tol/news/environment/article6087833.ece> (accessed 23 April, 2009).

BBC News, (18 March 2009), '"Armed" chimps go wild for honey'. Online. Available HTTP: <http://news.bbc.co.uk/1/hi/sci/tech/7946614.stm> (accessed 19 March, 2009).

BBC News (29 March 2007), 'Should apes have human rights?'. Online. Available HTTP: < http://news.bbc.co.uk/1/hi/magazine/6505691. stm> (accessed 11 September, 2008).

Benjamin, L. T & Bruce, D., (1982), 'From Bottle-Fed Chimp to Bottlenose Dolphin: A Contemporary Appraisal of Winthrop Kellogg', *The Psychological Record*, 32, pp. 461–482.

Bird, C. & Emery, N. J., (2009), 'Rooks Use Stones to Raise the Water Level to Reach a Floating Worm', *Current Biology*, 19 (16), pp. 1410–1414.

Bluff, L., Weir, A., Rutz, C., Wimpenny, J., and Kacelnik A., (2007), 'Tool-related Cognition in New Caledonian Crows', *Comparative Cognition and Behaviour reviews*, 2, pp. 1–25.

Brown, R., (1973) *A First Language: The early stages,* (Cambridge, MA: Harvard University Press).

Bryson, B., (2004), *A short history of nearly everything,* (London: Transworld Publishers).

Budiansky, S., (1998), *If a Lion Could Talk: How animals think,* (London: Phoenix).

Burling, R., (2005), *The Talking Ape: How language evolved*, (Oxford: Oxford University Press).

Byrne, R. (2006), *The Thinking Ape: Evolutionary origins of intelligence*, (Oxford: Oxford University Press).

Byrnes, S. (28 February 2008), 'Animal rights, human wrongs', *New Statesman*.

Call, J. & Tomasello, M., (2008a), 'Does the chimpanzee have a theory of mind? 30 years later', *Trends in Cognitive Sciences*, 12 (5), pp. 187–192.

Call, J. & Tomasello, M., (2008b), *The Gestural Communication of Apes and Monkeys*, (London: Lawrence Erlbaum).

Callaway, E. (22 July 2009), 'Apes may imitate but they struggle to innovate', *New Scientist*. Online. Available HTTP: <http://www. newscientist.com/article/dn17499-why-apes-may-imitate-but-will-never-innovate.html> (accessed 11 September, 2008).

Carpenter, M., and Call, J., (in press), 'Comparing the imitative skills of children and nonhuman apes', *Primatologie*.

Cavalieri, P. & Singer, P., (1993), *The Great Ape Project: Equality beyond humanity*, (London: Fourth Estate).

CBS News, (July 14, 1999), 'The Mother Of All Orangutans', *CBS News*, Online. Available HTTP: <http://www.cbsnews.com/stories/1999/07/14/48hours/main54343.shtml> (accessed 7 August, 2009).

Cheney, D.L. & Seyfarth, R.M., (1990), 'Attending to behaviour versus attending to knowledge: examining monkeys' attribution of mental states', *Animal Behaviour*, 40 (4), pp. 742–753.

Cummings, D., (2009), 'The depraved genius of John Calvin', *The spiked review of books*, 26. Online. Available HTTP: <http://www. spiked-online.com/index.php/site/reviewofbooks_article/7208/> (accessed 14 August, 2009).

Custance, D. M., Whiten, A., & Bard, K. A., (1995), 'Can young chimpanzees (Pan troglodytes) imitate arbitrary actions? Hayes and Hayes (1952) revisited'. *Behaviour*, pp. 132, 837–859.

Desilets, M., (2008), 'Single mother: Saving the lives of our closest cousins', *Scanorama*, May Issue, pp. 40–49.

de Waal, F. ,(2006), *Our Inner Ape: The best and worst of human nature* (London: Granta Books).

Diamond, J., (1988), *Guns, Germs and Steel: A short history of everybody for the last 13,000 years*, (London: Random House).

Donald, M., (2002), *A Mind So Rare*, (New York: Norton Paperback)

Donaldson, M. ,(1978), *Children's Minds*, (London: HarperCollins).

Dreifus, C., (14 April 1998), 'A Conversation: With Emily Sue Savage-Rumbaugh; She Talks to Apes and, According to Her, They Talk Back', *New York Times*, Online. Available HTTP: <http://www.geocities. com/RainForest/Vines/4451/SheTalks.html> (accessed 11 May, 2009).

Engels, F., (1982), *The Part Played by Labour in the Transition from Ape to Man*, (Moscow: Progress Publishers).

Fisher, J. & Hinde, R. A., (1949), 'The opening of milk bottles in birds', *Br. Birds.*, 42, pp. 347–357.

Foree, D. D., & Lolordo, V. M., (1973), 'Attention in the pigeon: Differential effects of food-getting versus shock-avoidance procedures', *Journal of Comparative and Physiological Psychology*, 85, pp. 551 –558.

Fossey, D., (1983), *Gorillas in the Mist*, (Boston: Mariner Books).

Freud, S., (2002), *Civilization and Its Discontents*, (London: Penguin Books).

Furedi, F., (2006), 'The Legacy of Humanism', in D. Cummings (ed.), *Debating Humanism*, (Exeter: Imprint Academic), pp. 22–29.

Galdikas, M.B., (1999), *Orangutan Odyssey*, (New York: Harry N. Abrams).

Galdikas, M.B., (1995), *Reflections of Eden: My years with the orangutans of Borneo*, (Newport Beach: Back Bay Books).

Galef, B. G. Jr., (1992), 'The question of animal culture', *Human Nature*, 3, pp.157–178.

Gallup, G.G., Anderson, J. R., Shillito, D.J., (2002), 'The Mirror Test', in M. Bekoff, C. Allen & G. Burghardt (Eds.), *The Cognitive Animal: Empirical and theoretical perspectives on animal cognition*, (Cambridge: MIT Press), pp. 325–33.

Gallup, G. G., Jr. (1970). Chimpanzees: Self-recognition. *Science*, 167, pp. 86–87.

Garcia, J. & Koelling, R. A., (1966), 'Relation of cue to consequence in avoidance learning', *Psychonomic Science*, 4, pp. 123–124.

Gergely, G., Bekkering, H., & Király, I., (2002), 'Rational imitation in preverbal infants'. *Nature*, 415, p. 755.

Glendinning, L., (26 June 2008), 'Spanish parliament approves "human rights" for apes', *The Guardian*. Online. Available HTTP: <http://www.guardian.co.uk/world/2008/jun/26/humanrights.anim alwelfare?gusrc=rss&feed=networkfront> (accessed 11 May, 2009).

Goodall, J., (1990), *Through a Window: Thirty years with the chimpanzees of Gombe*, (London: Penguin Books).

Goodall, J., (1971), *In the Shadow of Man*, (Boston: Houghton Mifflin).

Gray, J., (2002), *Straw Dogs: Thoughts on humans and other animals*, (London: Granta Books).

Griffin, D., R., (2001), *Animal Minds: Beyond cognition to consciousness*, (Chicago: University of Chicago Press).

Great Ape Project, (1993), Homepage. Online. Available HTTP: <http://www.greatapeproject.org/> (accessed 3 August, 2008).

Hanlon, M., (2007), *Ten Questions Science Can't Answer (Yet!): A guide to science's greatest mysteries*, (New York: Palgrave Macmillan).

Hare, B., Call, J. & Tomasello, M., (2001), 'Do chimpanzees know what conspecifics know?', *Animal Behaviour*, 61 (1), pp.139–151.

Hare, B., Call, J., Agnetta, B. & Tomasello, M., (2000), 'Chimpanzees know what conspecifics do and do not see', *Animal Behaviour*, 59 (4), pp. 771–85.

Harris, M., (1988), *Culture, People, Nature: An introduction to general anthropology* (New York: Thomas Y. Crowell).

Hayes, K., and Hayes, C., (1952), 'Imitation in a Home Raised Chimpanzee', *Journal of Comparative and Physiological Psychology*, 45, pp. 450–459.

Henderson, M., (10 March 2009), 'ANALYSIS: Chimp with malice on mind', *The Times*. Online. Available HTTP: <http://www.timesonline.co.uk/tol/news/uk/science/article5877804.ece> (accessed 19 March, 2009).

Henderson, M., (9 September 2008), 'How chimps' sympathetic hugs reflect our own, empathetic human behaviour', *The Times*. Online. Available HTTP: <http://www.timesonline.co.uk/tol/news/uk/science/article4710629.ece> (accessed 12 September, 2008).

Herrmann, E., Call, J., Hernàndez-Lloreda, M.V., Hare, B., Tomasello, M., (2007), 'Humans Have Evolved Specialized Skills of Social Cognition: The Cultural Intelligence Hypothesis', *Science*, 317 (5843), pp.1360–1366.

Heyes, C. M., (1994), 'Reflections on self-recognition in primates', *Animal Behaviour*, 47, pp. 909–919.

Highfield, R., (7 September 2007), 'Children outsmart chimps', *Daily Telegraph*, Online. Available HTTP: <http://www.telegraph.co.uk/scienceandtechnology/science/sciencenews/3305843/Children-outsmart-chimps.html > (accessed 3 August, 2008).

Hill, J. H., (1978), 'Apes and Language', *Annual Review of Anthropology*, 7, pp. 89–112.

Hobson, P., (2002), *The Cradle of Thought: Exploring the origins of thinking*, (London: Macmillan).

Horowitz, A., (2009), 'Disambiguating the "guilty look": Salient prompts to a familiar dog behaviour', *Behavioural Processes*, 81(3), pp. 447–452.

Humle, T. & Matsuzawa, T., (2002), 'Ant-dipping among the chimpanzees of Bossou, Guinea, and some comparisons with other sites', *American Journal of Primatology*, 58, pp. 133–148.

Humphrey, N., (19 August 1982), 'Consciousness: A just-so story', *New Scientist*, 95, pp. 473–477.

Hunt, G. R., (1996), 'Manufacture and use of hook-tools by New Caledonian crows', *Nature*, 379, pp. 249–251.

Hunt, G. R., & Gray, R. D., (2004), 'Direct observations of pandanus-tool manufacture and use by a New Caledonian crow (Corvus moneduloides)', *Animal Cognition*, 7, pp. 114–120.

Inoue, S. & Matsuzawa, T., (2007), 'Working memory of numerals in chimpanzees', *Current Biology*, 17, p 23.

Kacelnik, A., Chappell, J., Weir, A.A.S., and Kenward, B. (2006), 'Cognitive adaptations for tool-related behaviour in New Caledonian Crows', in E.A. Wasserman and T.R. Zentall (eds.) *Comparative Cognition: Experimental explorations of animal intelligence*, (London: Oxford University Press), pp. 515–528.

Keim, B., (14 October 2008), 'Chimps: Not Human, But Are They People?' *Wired Science*, Online. Available HTTP: <http://www. wired.com/wiredscience/2008/10/chimpanzees-not/> (accessed 25 June, 2009).

Keim, B., (3 December 2007), 'Are You Smarter Than a Chimpanzee?' *Wired Science*, Online. Available HTTP: <http://www.wired.com/ wiredscience/2007/12/are-you-smarter/> (accessed 25 June, 2009).

Kellogg, W. N., (1968), 'Communication and Language in the Home-Raised Chimpanzee', *Science*, 162 (3852), pp. 423–427.

Kellogg, W.N. & Kellogg, L.A., (1933), *The Ape and The Child: A comparative study of the environmental influence upon early behavior*, (New York: McGraw-Hill Book Co)

Kennedy, A., (26 August 2009), 'Civilisation: it's more than good culture', *spiked*. Online. Available HTTP: <http://www.spiked-online. com/index.php/site/article/7314/> (accessed 29 August, 2009).

Kristof, N., (8 April 2009), 'Humanity Even for Nonhumans', *New York Time*. Online. Available HTTP: <http://www.nytimes. com/2009/04/09/opinion/09kristof.html?_r=1&th&emc=th> (accessed 9 April, 2009).

Leggett, H., (2009), 'Clever Crows Prove Aesop's Fable Is More Than Fiction', *Wired Science*, 6 August, Online. Available HTTP: <http:// www.wired.com/wiredscience/2009/08/aesopscrows/> (accessed 29 August, 2009).

Lovett, J. C. & Marshall, A. R., (2006), 'Why should we conserve primates?', *African Journal of Ecology*, 44, pp. 1–5.

Lowenstein, J., (1 November 1992), 'Can We Wipe Out Disease?', *Discover: Science, Technology and the Future*. Online. Available HTTP: <http://discovermagazine.com/1992/nov/canwewipeoutdise150> (accessed 3 August, 2008).

Luria, A. R. & Vygotsky, L. S., (1992), *Ape, Primitive Man and Child,: Essays in the history of behavior*, (New York: Harvester Wheatsheaf).

Marquardt, K., (1995), 'Are Your Ready for Our New Age Future?', *Insider's Report*, (Washington, D.C.: American Policy Center).

Marshall-Pescini, S. & Whiten, A., (2008), 'Chimpanzees (Pan troglodytes) and the Question of Cumulative Culture: An experimental approach', *Animal Cognition*, 11, pp. 449–456.

Meltzoff, A. N., (2007), '"Like me": A foundation for social cognition', *Developmental Science*, 10 (1), pp. 126–134.

Miles, H.L., Mitchell, R.W. & Harper, S.E., (1996), 'Simon Says: The development of imitation in an enculturated orangutan', in A.E. Russon, K.A. Bard & S.T. Parker (Eds.), *Reaching into thought*, (Cambridge: Cambridge University Press), pp. 278–299.

Mithen, S., (1998), *The Prehistory of the Mind: A search for the origins of art, religion and science*, (London: Phoenix).

Morgan, C. L., (1903), *An Introduction To Comparative Psychology*, (Revised edition) (London: Walter Scott).

Moura, A. C. and Lee, P. C., (2004), 'Capuchin Stone Tool Use in Caatinga Dry Forest', *Science*, 306, (5703), p 1909.

Myowa-Yamakoshi, M., & Matsuzawa, T., (2000), 'Imitation of intentional manipulatory actions in chimpanzees (Pan troglodytes)', *Journal of Comparative Psychology*, 114, pp. 381–391.

Myowa-Yamakoshi, M., & Matsuzawa, T., (1999), 'Factors influencing imitation of manipulatory actions in chimpanzees', *Journal of Comparative Psychology*, 113, pp. 128–136.

Neisser, A., (1983), *The Other Side of Silence*, (New York: Knopf).

O'Neill, B., (16 September, 2008), 'Who will win the polar bear vote?', *spiked*, Online. Available HTTP: < http://www.spiked-online.com/index.php/site/article/5728/> (accessed 20 December, 2009).

Osvath, M., (2009), 'Spontaneous planning for future stone throwing by a male chimpanzee', *Current Biology*, 19 (5), pp. 190–191.

Parris, M., (30 August 2008), 'Nature superior to man? What green twaddle', *The Times*. Online. Available HTTP: <http://www.timesonline.co.uk/tol/comment/columnists/matthew_parris/article4636286.ece> (accessed 11 September, 2008).

Patterson, F. G. P., and Cohn, R. H., (1994), 'Self-recognition and self-awareness in lowland gorillas', in S. T. Parker and R. W. Mitchell and M. L. Boccia (eds.), *Self-awareness in animals and humans: developmental perspectives*, (New York: Cambridge University Press), pp. 273–290.

Penn, D., Holyoak, K., Povinelli, D., (2008), 'Darwin's mistake: Explaining the discontinuity between human and nonhuman minds', *Behavioral And Brain Sciences*, 31, pp. 109–178

Penn, D. & Povinelli, D., (2007a), 'Causal cognition in human and nonhuman animals: a comparative, critical review', *Annual Review of Psychology*, 58, pp. 97–118.

Penn, D. & Povinelli, D., (2007b), 'On the lack of evidence that non-human animals possess anything remotely resembling a "theory of mind"', *Philosophical Transactions of the Royal Society Biological Sciences*, 362 (1480), pp. 731–44.

Piaget, J., (1952), *The origins of intelligence in children*, (New York: International Universities Press).

Pickrell, J., (April 23, 2003), 'Crows Better at Tool Building Than Chimps, Study Says', *National Geographic News*, Online. Available HTTP: <http://news.nationalgeographic.com/news/2003/04/0423_030423_crowtools.html> (accessed 29 May, 2009).

Pinker, S., (1994), *The Language Instinct*, (London: Penguin).

Povinelli, D.J., (2004), 'Behind the Ape's Appearance: Escaping anthropomorhism in the study of other minds', *Daedalus: Journal of the American Academy of Arts and Sciences* , Winter, 29–41.

Povinelli, D.J., (2001), 'The minds of humans and apes are different outcomes of an evolutionary experiment', in S. Fitzpatrick & J. Bruer (Eds.), *Carving our Destiny: Scientific research faces a new millennium* (Washington, DC, National Academy of Sciences and John Henry Press), pp. 1–40.

Povinelli, D. J., (2000), *Folk Physics for Apes: The chimpanzee's theory of how the world works*, (New York: Oxford University Press)

Povinelli, D. J., (1996), 'What Chimpanzees (Might) Know about the Mind', in R. W. Wrangham, W. C. McGrew, F. B. M. de Waal, P. G. Heltne (eds.), *Chimpanzee Cultures*, (Harvard University Press), pp. 285–300.

Povinelli, D. J., Nelson, K. E., & Boyson, S. T., (1990), 'Inferences about guessing and knowing by chimpanzees (Pan troglodytes), *Journal of Comparative Psychology*, 104, pp. 203–10.

Povinelli, D. J. & Vonk, J., (2003), 'Chimpanzee minds: suspiciously human?', *Trends in Cognitive Sciences*, 7 (4), pp. 157–160.

Premack, D., (1988), '"Does the Chimpanzee Have a Theory of Mind?" Revisited' in R. W. Byrne & A. Whiten (eds.), *Machiavellian Intelligence*, (Oxford: Clarendon).

Premack, D. & Woodruff, G., (1978), 'Does the Chimpanzee Have a Theory of Mind?', *Behavioural and Brain Science*, 1 (4), pp. 515–26.

Repacholi, B. M., & Gopnik, A., (1997), 'Early reasoning about desires: Evidence from 14- and 18-month-olds', *Developmental Psychology*, 33 (1), pp. 12–21.

Richmond, B. G., Begun, D. R., Strait, D. S., (2001), 'Origin of Human Bipedalism: The knuckle-walking hypothesis revisited', *Yearbook Of Physical Anthropology*, 44, pp. 70–105.

Ross, S., (21 July 2008), 'Chimps Aren't Chumps', *New York Times*. Online. Available HTTP: <http://www.nytimes.com/2008/07/21/opinion/21ross.html> (accessed 3 August, 2008).

Ryder, R., (6 August 2005), 'All beings that feel pain deserve human rights', *The Guardian*. Online. Available HTTP: <http://www.guardian.co.uk/uk/2005/aug/06/animalwelfare> (accessed 1 September, 2008).

Sailer, S., (27 September 1999), 'Chimps and Chumps : What monkeys don't tell us about man', *National Review*.

Sample, I., (9 March 2009), 'Chimp who threw stones at zoo visitors showed human trait, says scientist', *The Guardian*. Online. Available HTTP: < http://www.guardian.co.uk/science/2009/mar/09/chimp-zoo-stones-science> (accessed 19 March, 2009).

Sanz, C., (4 March 2009), 'Design complexity in termite-fishing tools of chimpanzees (Pan troglodytes)', *Biology Letters*. Online. Available HTTP: <http://rsbl.royalsocietypublishing.org/content/firstcite/2009/02/27/rsbl.2008.0786.full> (accessed 20 March, 2009).

Scaife, M., & Bruner, J. S., (1975), 'The capacity for joint visual attention in the infant', *Nature*, 253, p 265.

Scaife, M & Bruner, J.S., (24 Jan 1975), 'The capacity for joint visual attention in the infant', *Nature*, 253, pp. 265–266.

Sebeok, T. A. & Umiker-Sebeok, J., (1979), 'Performing Animals: Secrets of the Trade', *Psychology Today*, p 91.

Seyfarth, R. M. & Cheney, D. L., (1982), 'How monkeys see the world: a review of recent research on East African Vervet monkeys', in C.T. Snowdon, C.H. Brown, and M.R. Petersen (eds.), *Primate Communication*, (Cambridge: Cambridge University Press).

Seyfarth, R. M., Cheney, D. L. and Marler, P., (1980), 'Monkey responses to three different alarm calls: evidence of predator classification and semantic communication', *Science*, 210, pp. 801–3.

Sherry, D. F. & Galef B. G., (1984), 'Cultural transmission without imitation: milk bottle opening by birds', *Animal Behaviour*, 32, pp.937–938.

Shriver, L., (24 May 2008), 'Earth would be very happy without humans', *Daily Telegraph*, Online. Available HTTP: <http://www.telegraph.co.uk/opinion/main.jhtml?xml=/opinion/2008/05/24/do2405.xml> (accessed 13 September, 2008).

Simmel, G., (1971), 'The Sociology of Sociability', in D.N. Levine (ed), *On Individuality and Social Forems*, (Chicago: Chicago University Press).

Singer, P., (2006), *In Defense of Animals*, (Oxford: Blackwell).

Singer, P., (19 May 2003), 'Some Are More Equal', *The Guardian*. Online. Available HTTP: < http://www.guardian.co.uk/uk/2003/may/19/animalwelfare.world > (accessed 23 October, 2008).

Singer, P., (1976), 'Animal Rights and Human Obligations: An Anthology', (New Jersey: Prentice-Hall).

Singer, P., (1975), *Animal Liberation: A new ethics for our treatment of animals*, (New York: Random House)

Skinner, B. F., (1974), *About Behaviorism*, (New York: Vintage Books).

Skinner, B. F., (1951), 'How to teach animals', *Scientific American*, 185(12), pp. 26–29.

Suarez, S., and Gallup, G. G., Jr., (1981), 'Self-recognition in chimpanzees and orangutans, but not gorillas', *Journal of Human Evolution*, 10, pp. 157–188.

Tallis, R., (2003), 'Escape from Eden', *New Humanist*, 118 (4).

Taylor, J., (2009), *Not a Chimp: The hunt to find the genes that make us human*, (Oxford: Oxford University Press.)

Tennie, C., Call, J. and Tomasello, M., (2009) 'Ratcheting up the ratchet: on the evolution of cumulative culture', *Philosophical Transactions of the Royal Society Biological Sciences*, 364 (1528), pp. 2405–2415.

Terrace, H., (1987), *Nim: A chimpanzee who learned sign language*, (Columbia University Press).

Terrace, H., (1981), 'A report to an academy, 1980', in T. A. Sebeok & R. Rosenthal (Eds.), *The Clever Hans Phenomenon: Communication with horses, whales, apes, and people*, Annals of the New York Academy of Sciences (364), pp. 94–114.

Terrace, H., (1979), 'How Nim Chimpsky Changed My Mind', *Psychology Today*, 13 (6), p 67.

Terrace, H., Petitto, L., Sanders, R., & Bever, T., (1979), 'Can an ape create a sentence?', *Science* (206), pp. 891–902.

The Gorilla Foundation, About The Gorilla Foundation, Online. Available HTTP: <http://www.koko.org/foundation/> (accessed 6 February, 2009).

Thorndike , E., (1911), *Animal Intelligence*, 48.

Time Magazine, (11 May 1998), *Love Drink Nipple Fake*, Online. Available HTTP: <http://www.time.com/time/magazine/article/0,9171,988326,00.html> (accessed 6 February, 2009).

Tomasello, M., (2008), *Origins of Human Communication*, (Cambridge, MA: MIT Press).

Tomasello, M., (May 25 2008), 'How Are Humans Unique?', *New York Times*.

Tomasello, M., (1999), *The Cultural Origin of Human Cognition*, (Cambridge, MA: Harvard University Press).

Tomasello, M., Call, J. & Hare, B., (2003), 'Chimpanzees understand psychological states – the question is which ones and to what extent', *Trends in Cognitive Sciences*, 7 (4), pp 153–156.

Tomasello, M., Davis-Dasilva, M., Camak, L. and Bard, K., (1987), 'Observational learning of tool-use by young chimpanzees', *Human Evolution*, 2 (2), pp. 175–183.

Tomasello, M., Savage-Rumbaugh, E. S. & Kruger, A. C., (1993), 'Imitative learning of actions on objects by children, chimpanzees, and enculturated chimpanzees', *Child Development*, 64, pp. 1688–1705.

Trevarthen, C., (1977), 'Descriptive Analyses of Infant Communicative Behaviour', in H.R. Schaffer (ed.), *Studies in Mother-Infant Interaction*, (London: Academic Press), pp. 227–270.

Trevarthen C., Aitken K.J., (2001), 'Infant Intersubjectivity: Research, Theory, and Clinical Applications', *Journal of Child Psychology and Psychiatry*, 42 (1), pp. 3–48.

Trevarthen, C. and Reddy, V., (2007), 'Consciousness in infants', in M. Velman & S. Schneider (Eds.), *A Companion to Consciousness*, (Oxford: Blackwells), pp. 41–57.

Tronick, E. Z., (2005), 'Why is Connection with Others so Critical? The Formation of Dyadic States of Consciousness: Coherence governed selection and the co-creation of meaning out of messy meaning making', in J. Nadel and D. Muir (eds), *Emotional development*, (Oxford: Oxford University Press), pp. 293– 315.

UN News Centre (1 December 2008), 'Africa-wide UN action plan seeks to save the gorilla', Online. Available HTTP: <http://www.un.org/apps/news/story.asp?NewsID=29137&Cr=Gorillas&Cr1=UNEP> (accessed 13 January, 2009).

van Schaik C.P., Ancrenaz, M., Borgen, G., Galdikas, B., Knott, C.D., Singleton, I., Suzuki, A., Utami S.S., Merrill, M., (2003), 'Orangutan cultures and the evolution of material culture', *Science*, 299, pp. 102–105.

Visalberghi, E., (2002), 'Insights from Capuchin Monkeys' Studies: ingredients of, recipes for, and flaws in capuchins' success', in M. Bekoff, C. Allen & G. Burghardt (Eds.), *The Cognitive Animal: Empirical and theoretical perspectives on animal cognition*, (Cambridge: MIT Press), pp. 405–411.

Visalberghi, E. & Limongelli, L., (1994), 'Lack of understanding of cause-effect relations in tool-using capuchin monkeys (*Cebus Apella*)', *Journal of Comparative Psychology*, 108, pp. 15–22.

Visalberghi, E. & Tomasello, M., (1998), 'Primate causal understanding of the physical and psychological domains', *Behavioural Processes*, 42, pp. 189–203.

Vonk, J. & Povinelli, D.J., (2006), 'Similarity and Difference in the Conceptual Systems of Primates: The Unobservability hypothesis', in E. Wasserman and T. Zentall (Eds.), *Comparative Cognition:*

Experimental explorations of animal intelligence, (Oxford University Press), pp. 363–387.

Vygotsky, L.S., (1986), *Thought and Language,* (Cambridge: The MIT Press).

Vygotsky, L.S., (1978), *Mind in Society: Development of higher psychological processes,* (Cambridge: Harvard University Press).

Wallman, J., (1992), *Aping Language,* (Cambridge: Cambridge University Press).

Weir, A.A.S., Chappell, J. and Kacelnik, A., (2002), 'Shaping of Hooks in New Caledonian Crows', *Science,* 297 (5583), p 981.

Wells, S., (3 July 2003), 'The great leap', *The Guardian.* Online. Available HTTP: < http://www.guardian.co.uk/education/2003/jul/03/research.highereducation1> (accessed 13 May, 2009).

Whiten, A., (2000), 'Primate Culture and Social Learning', *Cognitive Science,* 24 (3), pp. 477 – 508.

Whiten, A., (1996), 'Imitation, Pretence and Mindreading: Secondary representation in comparative primatology and developmental psychology?', in A. W. Russon, K. A. Bard, & S. T. Parker (Eds.), *Reaching into Thought: The minds of the great apes,* (Cambridge: Cambridge University Press), pp. 300–324.

Whiten, A., McGuigan, N., Marshall-Pescini, S. and Hopper, L., (2009), 'Emulation, imitation, over-imitation and the scope of culture for child and chimpanzee', *Philosophical Transactions of the Royal Society Biological Sciences,* 364, pp. 2417–2428.

Whiten, A., Spiteri, A., Horner, V., Bonnie, K. E., Lambeth, S. P., Schapiro, S., de Waal, F. B. M., (2007), 'Transmission of Multiple Traditions within and between Chimpanzee Groups', *Current Biology,* 17, pp. 1038–1043.

Whiten, A. & van Schaik, C. P. (2007), 'The evolution of animal 'cultures' and social intelligence', *Philosophical Transactions of the Royal Society,* 362 (1480), pp. 603–620.

Whiten, A., Goodall, J., McGrew, W.C., Nishida, T., Reynolds, V., Sugiyama, Y., Tutin, C.E.G., Wrangham, R.W., Boesch, C., (1999), 'Cultures in chimpanzees', *Nature,* 399, pp. 682–685.

Wood, D., (1989), 'Social interaction as tutoring', in M. H. Bornstein and J. S. Bruner (eds.), *Interaction in Human Development,* (Hillsdale, NJ: Lawrence Erlbaum Associates), pp 59–80.

Index

A Mind So Rare
    see Donald, Merlin
Adams, Douglas, 5, 12
Agnetta, Bryan, 73
Aitken, Kenneth, 62
American Sign Language (apes),
    83–90
An Essay on Man
    see Pope, Alexander
Animal Liberation
    see Singer, Peter
*Animal Minds: Beyond cognition
    to science*
    see Griffin, Donald
*Animal Rights and Human
    Obligations*
    see Singer, Peter
animals
    celebrity endorsement of
        rights, 1–2
    obsession with welfare, 4
    rights, 1–4, 2, 11, 109
    (un)ethical treatment of, 1
anthropocentrism, 2
    see also human distinctiveness
anthropomorphism, 7, 15–16, 76,
    91, 111
Ape, Primitive Man and Child
    see Luria, Alexander
        Romanovich
Aping Language
    see Wallman, Joel

associative learning, 20–22
Attenborough, David, 5

Benjamin, Ludy, 64
Bentham, Jeremy, 109
Bersani, Leo, 112
Biology Letters, 52
bipedalism, 100
Bird, Christopher, 47
Blackburn, Simon, 10
Blackmore, Susan, 5
Blakemore, Colin, 9
Bluff, Lucas, 48
Borsecnik, Katherine, 90
brain size, 99, 100, 102
Brecht, Bertolt, 45
Brown, Roger, 93
Bruce, Darryl, 64
Bruner, Jerome, 61
Bryson, Bill
    *A Short History of Nearly
        Everything*, 99
Budiansky, Stephen, 19, 23, 24
    If a Lion Could Talk, 19
Burling, Robbins, 79, 93
    *The Talking Ape: How language
        evolved*, 80, 98
Byrne, Richard, 22, 42, 52–53,
    70, 71, 72, 103
    *The Thinking Ape: Evolutionary
        origins of intelligence*, 22, 32

Call, Josep, 41, 72, 73, 74
   The Gestural Communication of
      Apes and Monkeys, 105
Carpenter, Melinda, 41
Cavalieri, Paola, 11
cave paintings, 104
cheap food, 4
Cheney, Dorothy, 81, 82
children, 40, 63–66
   cognition, 60, 107
   consciousness, 26, 57–58, 59,
      61, 62–63, 67, 72
   early infants, 59–63
   imitation, 39, 42, 60, 60–61
   language, 93, 94
   self awareness, 77
   sentence construction, 92
Children and Emotion: The
   development of psychological
   understanding
   see Harris, Paul
Chimpanzee and Human
   Communication Institute, 11
cognition
   collective, 96, 97
   human, 37, 107, 108
communication, animals, 79–81
consciousness
   apes, 59, 72
   children, 71
   chimpanzee, 71
   human, 25
   of observable and
      unobservable behaviour,
      73, 75
Cradle of Thought: Exploring the
   origins of thinking, The
   see Hobson, Peter
Cultural Origins of Human
   Cognition, The
   see Tomasello, Michael
cultural transmission, 105
   apes, 43, 46

humans, 43
primates, 32–33, 39
see also culture
culture
   capacity for in apes, 38
   cave paintings, 104
   collective, 96, 111
   creativity, 104
   'cultural sparks', 104
   'cultural take off', 103
   'cultural tools', 64
   cultural transmission, 105
   evolution, 45
   human, 58, 113
   learning of, 57
   'ratchet effect', 38
   see also cultural transmission
Cummings, Dolan, 113
Current Biology, 17
Custance, Deborah, 42

Daily Telegraph, 6
de Waal, Frans, 27, 29
   Our Inner Ape: The past and
      future of human nature, 27,
      28, 68
deception, apes, 70–71
Diamond, Jared
   Guns, Germs and Steel, 102,
      103
Discover, 5
'Disneyfying' animals, 7
   see also anthropomorphism
DNA
   see genetics
Does the Chimpanzee Have a
   Theory of the Mind?
   see Premack, David;
      Woodruff, Guy
Dog Whisperer, The
   see Millan, Cesar
Donald, Merlin
   A Mind So Rare, 96, 112

eidectic memory, 18
Emery, Nathan, 47
empathy, 68
emulation, 34, 36, 37, 39, 41, 45
    see also social learning;
    stimulus enhancement
'encultured apes' (raised by
    humans), 41
Engels, Friedrich, 30
    *The Part Player by Labour in
    the Transition from Ape to
    Man*, 30, 99
evolution, 95, 97, 98–99, 101, 103
    influence of natural
    environmental changes on,
    100–101

factory farming, 9
Fearnley-Whittingstall, Hugh, 1
*Folk Physics for Apes: The
    chimpanzee's theory of how the
    world works*
    see Povinelli, Daniel
Fossey, Dian, 12, 13, 14
    Dian Fossey Gorilla Fund
    International, 14
    Gorillas in the Mist, 13
Fouts, Deborah, 11
Fraser, Orlaith, 68
Freud, Sigmund
    Civilisation and its Discontents,
    112
Fukuyama, Francis, 29
Our Posthuman Future, 29
Furedi, Frank, 113
Furness, William, 83

Galdikas, Biruté, 12, 14
    Orangutan Odyssey, 15
    *Reflections of Eden: My years
    with the orangutans of
    Borneo*, 14
Galef, Bennett, 33
Gallup, Gordon, 76–77

    see also mirror recognition
Gardner, Allen, 83, 88
Gardner, Beatrix, 83, 88
genetics, 12, 18, 27, 97
Gergely, György, 60
*Gestural Communication of Apes
    and Monkeys, The*
    see Call, Josep; Tomasello,
    Michael
Goodall, Jane, 12, 13
    *Through a Window: Thirty
    years with the chimpanzees
    of Gombe*, 69
Gopnik, Alison, 67
Gorilla, United Nations Year of
    the, 2
Gorillas in the Mist
    see Fossey, Dian
Gray, John, 5, 7
    *Straw Dogs: Thoughts on
    humans and other animals*, 5
Great Ape Project (GAP), 2, 3,
    5, 11, 12
Griffin, Donald, 23, 34
    *Animal Minds: Beyond
    cognition to science*, 23
    Clever Hans case, 23–24
Guardian, 16
Guns, Germs and Steel
    see Diamond, Jared

Hanlon, Michael, 3, 75–76, 96
    *Ten Questions Science Can't
    Answer (Yet!)*, 3, 110
Hare, Brian, 73, 74, 75
Harris, Marvin, 103
Harris, Paul, 66
    *Children and Emotion: The
    development of psychological
    understanding*, 66
Hayes, Catherine, 41, 42, 83
Hayes, Keith, 83
Henderson, Mark, 68
Herrmann, Esther, 26, 59, 107

Heyes, Cecilia, 77
Hill, Jane, 86
Hobson, Peter, 61, 63
  The Cradle of Thought:
  Exploring the origins of
  thinking, 61
hominids, 100, 101
Homo erectus, 99, 102
Homo habilis, 101
Homo sapiens sapiens, 56–57,
  99, 100, 101, 102, 104
Horowitz, Alexandra
  anthropomorphism (pet
  dogs), 15–16
human distinctiveness, 37, 38,
  40, 43, 54–55, 56–58, 94, 100,
  103, 108, 113–114
  cognition, 107
  cultural, 97
  'cultural take off', 104
  genetic, 97
  social language, 104
  social transmission, 105
  unobservable events, 106
  see also collective cognition;
    culture; Vygotsky, Lev
    Semyonovich
human uniqueness
  see anthropocentrism; human
    distinctiveness
humanism
  see anthropocentrism; human
    distinctiveness; humanity
humanity
  common, 111
  degraded view of, 4–7
  history making potential, 29
  value of, *vis a vis* animals, 7
Humphrey, Nicholas, 106
Hunt, Gavin, 47

If a Lion Could Talk
  see Budiansky, Stephen
imitation, 34–35, 39, 41, 42

apes, 40
children, 60, 64
early infants, 63
human, 56
innovation
  apes, 45
International Journal of
  Primatology, 17

James, William, 78
Johanson, Donald, 101
Joint Attention Episodes, 61,
  62, 63

Kacelnik, Alex, 48, 49
Kellogg, Luella, 63–64, 83
Kellogg, Winthrop, 63–64, 83
Kennedy, Angus, 30–31
Kruger, Ann Cale, 41

language, 80
  American Sign Language
    (apes), 83–90
  apes, 84, 86, 87, 90–92
  children, 93, 94 *see*
    also Vygotsky, Lev
    Semyonovich
  chimpanzee, 83, 87–88, 89
  'cultural take off', 104
  emergence, 98
  gorillas, 85
  'linguistic take off', 103
  orangutan, 83, 85
  social language, 104
Language Instinct, The
  see Pinker, Steven
Leakey, Louis, 12
Life After People (TV
  documentary), 6
Limongelli, Luca, 51
linguistic ability
  see language
Lowenstein, Professor Jerold, 5
Lucanus, Terentius, 1

Luria, Alexander Romanovich,
56, 57, 94
Ape, Primitive Man and Child,
56
see also Vygotsky, Lev
Semyonovich

Machiavellian intelligence, 69
Manifesto Club, 113
Marshall-Pescini, Sarah, 40
Marx, Karl, 29
Matsuzawa, Tetsuro, 17–18
Max Planck Institute for
Evolutionary Biology, 26, 35,
37, 41, 43, 52, 59, 72, 107
Meltzoff, Andrew, 60
Middle/Upper Palaeolithic
period, 104
Miles, Lynn, 85
Millan, Cesar, 24
The Dog Whisperer, 24
mimicry
see imitation
mirror recognition, 76–78
Mithen, Steven, 30, 31–32, 46,
92, 100, 102, 104
*The Prehistory of the Mind:
A search for the origins of
art, religion and science*, 30,
58, 98
Morgan, Conway Lloyd, 19–20
motor skills, 63

National Geographic, 14, 47
National Review, 19
Nature, 61
New Scientist, 39, 106
New Statesman, 9
New York Times, 3, 4, 79
New Yorker, 13
Nielsen, Lone Drøscher, 6
*Nim: A chimpanzee who learned
sign language*
see Terrace, Herbert

*Not a Chimp: the hunt for genes
that make us human*
see Taylor, Jeremy

O'Neill, Brendan, 2
Optimum Population Trust, 5
Orangutan Odyssey
see Galdikas, Biruté
*Origins of Human
Communications*
see Tomasello, Michael
Osvath, Mathias, 17
*Our Inner Ape: The past and
future of human nature*
see de Waal, Frans
Our Posthuman Future
see Fukuyama, Francis

Palaeolithic revolution, 102
Parris, Matthew, 4
*Part Player by Labour in the
Transition from Ape to Man,
The*
see Engels, Friedrich
Patterson, Dr. Penny, 85
Pavlov, Ivan, 20–21
Penn, Derek, 43, 54, 75
People for the Ethical Treatment
of Animals (PETA), 1
photographic memory
see eidectic memory
Piaget, Jean, 26
symbolic thinking, 26–27
Pinker, Steven, 92–93
The Language Instinct, 90, 91
polar bear, as symbol of
destruction of the planet, 2
Pope, Alexander, 11
An Essay on Man, 11
Povinelli, Daniel, 53, 54, 55, 71,
72, 75, 98, 105, 106
chimpanzee and human
intelligence, 16
Folk Physics for Apes: The

*chimpanzee's theory of how
the world works*, 53
Prehistory of the Mind, The
see Mithen, Steven
Premack, David, 65
*Does the Chimpanzee Have a
Theory of the Mind?*, 65
primatology, 14
Prince Philip, HRH, 5

Rapocholi, Betty, 67
'ratchet effect', in human
culture, 38
*Reflections of Eden: My years with
the orangutans of Borneo*
see Galdikas, Biruté
Royal Society for the Prevention
of Cruelty to Animals
(RSPCA), 2
Rumbaugh, Duane, 84
Rutz, Christian, 48
Ryder, Richard, 2

Sailer, Steve, 19
Sanz, Crickette, 52
Savage-Rumbaugh, Sue, 41, 79,
84, 92
Scaife, Michael, 61
see also Joint Attention
Episodes
Schriver, Lionel, 6
Science, 26, 87
Sebeok, Thomas, 91
self awareness
apes, 77–78
human, 78
Seligman, Martin, 22–23
Seyfarth, Robert, 81, 82
Simmel, George, 112
Singer, Peter, 2, 11, 111, 112
Animal Liberation, 3, 109
*Animal Rights and Human
Obligations*, 110
In Defense of Animals, 4

*Great Ape Project: Equality
beyond humanity*, 95
Skinner, B.F., 21
associative learning, 20
social intelligence, apes, 67
social learning, 45, 105
apes, 46
children, 41, 60–61
chimpanzees, 41
see also emulation; stimulus
enhancement
speciesism, 2, 110
spiked, 30–31
stimulus enhancement, 33–34,
45, 50
see also emulation; social
learning
*Straw Dogs: Thoughts on humans
and other animals*
see Gray, John

*Talking Ape: How language
evolved, The*
see Burling, Robbins
Tallis, Raymond, 7
Taylor, Jeremy, 18
*Not a Chimp: The hunt for
genes that make us human*,
10, 18–19, 49, 109
*Ten Questions Science Can't
Answer (Yet!)*
see Hanlon, Michael
Tennyson, Alfred Lord, 9
Terrace, Herbert, 86, 87, 88, 89
*Nim: A chimpanzee who learned
sign language*, 86
Theory of Mind, 65, 66, 71, 75
apes, 68–69, 72
*Thinking Ape: Evolutionary origins
of intelligence, The*
see Byrne, Richard
Thorndike, Edward, 21
*Through a Window: Thirty years
with the chimpanzees of Gombe*
see Goodall, Jane

Time, 90
Tomasello, Michael, 37, 41, 43,
　45, 46, 52, 57, 58, 72, 73, 74,
　105, 107
　*The Cultural Origins of Human
　　Cognition*, 45, 103
　*The Gestural Communication of
　　Apes and Monkeys*, 105
　*Origins of Human
　　Communications*, 82
tools
　human use, 47, 102, 103
　role in human
　　distinctiveness, 99
　use of by apes, 12, 31, 38, 45,
　　47, 51, 52, 53, 54
Trevarthen, Colwyn, 62

Uhlenbroek, Charlotte, 67
Umiker-Sebeok, Jean, 91
Upper Palaeolithic age, 103
van Schaik, Carel, 45

Visalberghi, Elisabetta, 50–51,
　52
Vonk, Jennifer, 72, 105, 106
Vygotsky, Lev Semyonovich, 56,
　57, 94
　Ape, Primitive Man and Child,
　　56

Wallman, Joel, 80–81, 92
　Aping Language, 89, 91
Weir, Alex, 47
Wells, Spencer, 101
Whiten, Andrew, 31, 38, 39, 40,
　45
WildAid, 2
Wimpenny, Joanna, 48
Wired, 17
Wood, David, 35
Woodruff, Guy, 65
　*Does the Chimpanzee Have a
　　Theory of the Mind?*, 65